Collins

need to know?

Property

Kate Faulkner

Collins

First published in 2006 by Collins
an imprint of
HarperCollins Publishers
77-85 Fulham Palace Road
London W6 8JB

www.collins.co.uk

09 08 07 06
5 4 3 2 1

A catalogue record for this book is available from
the British Library

Managing editor: Emma Callery
Editor: Kate Parker
Designer: Bob Vickers
Series design: Mark Thomson
Front cover photograph: © Getty Images/Sam Roberts
Back cover photographs: Nikki English

ISBN-13 978-0-00-720-776-3
ISBN-10 0-00-720-776-X

Colour reproduction by Colourscan, Singapore
Printed and bound by Printing Express Ltd,
Hong Kong

Contents

Introduction 6

1 **How to value a property** 13

2 **How to choose the right services** 41

3 **Planning and preparing to move** 83

4 **Structure and layout** 121

5 **Renting a property** 151

Glossary 185

Further addresses 188

Index 190

Introduction

The UK is passionate about property. Owning our own home is one of our highest priorities, at the top of many of our 'wish' lists. According to the latest European Commission report, over 69% of us buy rather than rent.

People's attitudes to property have changed over the last few years. In the late 1980s, property prices plummeted and, for the first time, many people realized that property was not the guaranteed investment it had been in the past. This view has changed again as prices have soared since 1998. As a result of these ups and downs in prices over the last 15 years, some see property as an investment and a good way to build a pension, while others fear prices may crash again. The real truth is no one is quite sure which view is right.

Despite our love of property, most of our experience in buying and selling it leads us to regard it as an extremely stressful process. Considering the importance of a property as an asset – often our chief financial asset – coupled with the reasons why we tend to move and how we go about the process, this is hardly surprising.

For example, we often have to move because of major changes in our personal circumstances. This might be leaving home, getting married, having a baby, or because changes in the family mean that downsizing or upsizing is necessary. We may be getting divorced, for instance, or are moving because of the loss of a loved one. Add in selling a property we have typically lived in for many years and moving all our possessions, it is all too clear why moving is such a stressful business.

However, there are two tricks that will make your life much easier when moving home. The first is to gain a real understanding of the local housing market. When buying or selling a property, we tend to spend most of our time assessing

assessing the market we are buying in, not the one we are selling in. This is one of the first mistakes people make, as most of us have to sell our home in order to afford a new one. It is much more important to consider first of all the value of the property we need to sell, how many people are likely to want to buy it and how long it may take to sell. Only once we have this information can we truly know what we can afford.

Generally, we would much prefer to buy rather than rent. But renting might be our only option, or an option to consider if we think moving might otherwise be difficult. For example, at any one time in the whole of the UK there are 200,000–300,000 properties on the market, and double that number of people potentially looking for a new home. That means there can be a limited supply of properties to choose from. A three-bedroom, semi-detached house on an estate may sell very quickly, for example, and it may be easy to find a four-bedroom detached property in the area, but if you are looking for a 200-year-old farmhouse, for instance, it may not be on the market when you want to buy, so renting in between can be a sensible option.

Once you have gained an understanding of the local housing market, the second trick to moving home successfully is to choose the right companies to help with your move. Many of the services you need are not regulated, so it is important to understand how to pick the right company to work with and how much it will cost so that you know how much to spend on removal costs and furnishing/renovating your new home.

The aim of this book is to give you a better understanding of how the property market works. The following chapters cover important facts, figures and other information to help you gain a proper insight into the local market you are buying, selling or renting in, so that you can make the right decisions. And being well prepared in this way should hopefully take some of the stress out of your house move.

Key property types in the UK

Everyone has a different view of what would be their ideal property. It might be a modern city apartment, a thatched cottage, a Georgian mansion, a Victorian terrace or even a log cabin in the middle of nowhere. Fortunately property in the UK can cater for a wide range of tastes.

The history of property

Property in this country has an extremely diverse history and because some of the old building techniques weather so well, many old houses are still around today. In addition, 'character' properties can make a good investment as they typically command higher prices on the housing market. The downside is that, by definition, they tend to be in much shorter supply than newer properties.

Before you buy, it is important to think through the type of property you want as well as how many bedrooms or reception rooms you need. And it is important to keep an open mind. For example, if you are after a two- or three-bedroom property with a large garden, you might specify a house to an estate agent, whereas a bungalow is likely to have sufficient space as well as a large garden.

If you have a fixed idea of what it is you want, however, then research the market for that specific type of property and check the pros and cons of owning it (as outlined in Chapter 4). If the type of property you're after is in short supply, you may be better off selling your home first and then making offers when you know exactly how much money you have to spend.

Below is an overview of some of the key property types in the UK that you are likely to come across. You could use this section to help define the types of property you are willing to consider when briefing an estate agent.

Timber-framed houses and thatched cottages

Most of these properties date were built prior to the 19th century and they were constructed from local materials, using local skills. Timber-framed houses were built from around the Norman times until the Tudor age and therefore date back to around the 15th century and earlier. They are extremely difficult to find and command high prices. Thatched cottages date from a little later, from the 18th century, and may be found throughout the UK, mostly in villages or rural communities.

Georgian properties

These date back to the 18th century. They were generally built in the town centre itself and on the outskirts, or as large houses in the countryside. Many of the houses were designed for the wealthy, so they tend to be large, with two to three storeys and elegantly proportioned rooms and windows. They can be found in old cities and market towns such as London, Bath and Colchester and their surrounding areas. But as few such properties have gardens or parking places, it is important to think about the practicalities of living in one if you have young children.

Victorian houses

The Victorian age (1837–1901) was a great time for house building. One of the differences between the Victorian and Georgian period is that Victorian properties came in more shapes and sizes. There are two-up, two-down terraces and up to four- or five-bedroom (or more) detached properties. Typically, Victorian houses were built in roads off the town centre and further out, creating some of the first suburbs. Something to be aware of with Victorian terraces is that some were built with 2+1 bedrooms, meaning the third bedroom is only accessed through the second bedroom and many only have a bathroom downstairs.

Bungalows

Bungalows started to appear in the UK in the late 19th century, emulating the colonialist style of living on one floor, and have continued to be built ever since. They can be found across the UK and range in size from small, one-bedroom properties, usually on a housing estate, to large, 'one-off' homes with 4–5 bedrooms and huge gardens – although all bungalows tend to be located on a good-sized plot. Typically of brick construction, most have large loft spaces, which is good for storage or for extending into the loft (for which you may need planning permission, however).

In the past, bungalows have been regarded as a property for older people who find it difficult to get up and down the stairs. However, as property prices have gone up and the choice of good-value property has become more restricted, this type of house is proving increasingly popular for younger people and families looking for larger gardens or for properties that can be extended.

Edwardian properties

The Edwardian era of building (1901–20) was fairly short. Hence there are not a vast number of such properties in existence and so they can command a higher price than equivalent Victorian houses. Properties from this period tended to be built for the wealthy – big houses with wide frontages and generous accommodation.

1930s semi-detached houses

Semi-detached houses from the 1930s are of standard construction and very well built. They can be seen in the suburbs of most major towns and cities. They are usually found on main roads into towns or on leafy housing estates. They vary in size, but most have 3–4 bedrooms with spacious gardens.

Social housing

After the Second World War, local councils built masses of properties, from the infamous high-rise blocks to three-bedroom semis on housing estates. Then during the 1980s large numbers of these properties were sold off. As a result, many are now privately owned and can represent good-value housing, as most are well built, with decent-sized rooms and gardens, and often situated near to local amenities. Since the 1980s, housing associations have taken over the building of social housing from the local councils. These now manage tenants, offer shared ownership and even sell parts of their portfolio to private owners (see page 146–7).

Loft and apartment living

In the 1990s, planning permission started to place restrictions on the land that property developers could build on, and so they turned to brownfield sites. Derelict industrial districts with large brick-built warehouses or factories were either pulled down or converted to create loft and penthouse apartments, encouraging people back to the city and helping to improve run-down areas. Such properties have led to the rise of 'open-plan' living with expensive loft and penthouse apartments, through to smaller one- and two-bedroom flats. The flats tend to offer one or two parking spaces, good security and even built-in leisure complexes and concierge services.

21st-century developments

Because of the demand for smaller homes, private builders now have to build more 'mixed developments', which means that a range of property sizes must be offered in order to gain planning permission rather than a development consisting solely of larger, more profitable properties. So if you are looking at buying 'new', then you are likely to find a property on an estate consisting of different-sized houses, although usually without such a good-sized garden as an older property because of the restriction that there is on space today.

1 How to value a property

We constantly see newspaper headlines proclaiming 'property market crashing' or 'average house prices go through the roof'. The problem with the property 'market' is that it is actually made up of many different types of property across different areas of the UK. And the problem with the term 'average house price' is that there is no such thing as an 'average' house. So how do we actually work out what is happening in the property market and, based on this information, assess the value of the property we wish to sell and the one we want to buy?

House prices since 1970

To understand how to use the information that you need to assess the value of your own property and a property you are going to buy, it is important to see how house prices have changed in the past.

The 'yo-yo' effect

Since 1970, the average house price appears to have grown dramatically. What you need to know is how prices move historically so that you can assess current price movements in relation to the sale/purchase of your own property. The first thing to realize is that the whole process, from the time you think of selling a property to the time you actually sell, buy and move home, takes anything from a few months to a year or more. During this time property prices can go up, down, stay the same or do all three!

In fact, prices do not just go up and up and then suddenly crash back down. Instead they 'yo-yo'. Sometimes they can go up every quarter or year, after which they might stay static or fall for a short time then recover. It is only really in the late 1980s and early 1990s that the market fell sharply and took longer to recover.

What is important to learn from this information is that although property prices may have fallen from time to time, they have rarely

---

must know

The property market

▶ The property market can go down over a few months or by a quarter. When this happens, the media will start reporting adverse headlines and talking about a 'crash', but if you are buying or selling at the time it does not necessarily mean that a crash is actually on its way. For this to happen the market needs to consistently fall over a long period of time.

▶ The average property price has grown from £5,000 in 1970 to over £150,000 in 2004. Although all prices have increased over this time, property has increased more than most. Property market prices over time have risen virtually every quarter and every year since this time, apart from the serious crash in the late 1980s and early 1990s.

'crashed'. Even if they do crash, it may then take a number of months, or even years, for prices to pick up again, but the overall trend over the past three decades has been for house prices to rise.

So why did house prices crash in the late 1980s?

The property market rose dramatically during the 1980s. Then, in the summer of 1989, prices peaked and started to fall. This fall continued for the next four years and prices did not recover to their pre-summer 1989 level until 1998 – nearly ten years later.

The reasons for house-price movements are always complex, but the key reason that prices suddenly stopped rising was because average house prices exceeded the threshold that people were able to afford based on the restricted income multiples that the lenders would agree to. In the 1980s, the rules governing the amount one could borrow to buy a property were very strict compared to today. Lenders typically lent three and a half times a single income or two to two and half times a dual income. In addition, interest rates in 1988 were around 8.5% and mortgage repayments accounted for less than 20% of our household expenditure. The average house price to earnings ratio at this time was 5:2.

In its own right, this may have halted the growth of house prices, but should not necessarily have caused them to drop so suddenly or by so much. But economic conditions changed too and interest rates started to rise, peaking at nearly 16%. The result was devastating to homeowners. The increased cost of a mortgage meant that 30% of income was now taken up with the cost of ownership. For some people, this was just unaffordable. They couldn't keep up with payments, so their properties were repossessed and lenders needed to sell them at any cost to recoup their money. But people were not buying as readily; they were waiting for prices to bottom out. In short, there were few buyers

good to know

Factors preventing a downturn in property prices
There are several reasons why current property prices seem to have defied the 'doom and gloom' scenario so far:

Changes in lending from income multiples to 'affordability'
Lenders now approve mortgage levels based on household income and expenditure. In the late 1980s, if you had an annual salary of £25,000 then the maximum a lender would give would be £87,500. Today, on a salary of £25,000 and if you have a company car and no dependants, you could borrow £135,000 – equating to 5.4 times your salary.

First-time buyers being given 'a helping hand'
Despite being able to borrow more money, the increase in the deposit required should also have prevented many first-time buyers from being able to purchase a property. But, because many parents and grandparents can afford to lend or give the additional money, first-time buyers have continued to buy. Many second-time buyers would not have been able to buy, either, as they could not have raised the required 10% deposit at the time of exchange, but because of the price rises, most sellers now accept only a 5% deposit.

Increased number of buy-to-let investors
In the late 1980s, first-time buyers could not afford to buy. If no one buys at the 'bottom' of a house-price chain, then no one else in the chain can move either. Although the number of first-time buyers has been decreasing over the last few years, which would normally cause house prices to slow down, buy-to-let investors have replaced them, allowing the market to rise.

Interest rates at an all-time low
Contrary to the late 1980s, interest rates are at an all-time low, so this has allowed price increases to continue. However, interest rate rises during 2004 appear to have caused the longest halt to house-price growth since 1998.

Shortage of housing stock
In the UK, we are building fewer homes a year than in Europe, yet we need more properties than ever before. Our need for smaller, single-occupancy homes is increasing. We are living longer, have more single-parent families and are marrying later, yet in some areas we don't even have enough land to build on. Demand for property therefore remains high, while property stocks in comparison are at an all-time low.

and lots of properties on the market. Prices continued to drop until the property stock that was on the market started to match the demand.

But people have to move house, whatever the economic conditions. They get married, have children or change jobs, so back in the 1990s properties still had to be sold and bought and properties that were priced correctly did sell. It was not until the economy started to pick up and interest rates began to fall once again that the confidence returned and the property market began to recover.

Will the market crash again?

Over the last few years, many have suggested that the property market is 'overpriced' and that we are heading for another crash – just as we did in the 1980s. Some experts, such as Capital Economics, a London-based consultancy, believe that the market will decline by up to 30%, while others are predicting a slowdown in the housing market with prices staying level or declining by a few per cent until average income growth catches up with recent growth in the average house price.

How can you work out which prediction is right?

We have already seen (see page 14) how the market can take a downturn in a month or a quarter, but to understand whether this is likely to be a 'blip' or a crash, you need to know what drives property prices up and down.

The 'doom and gloom' scenario is mainly based on the lessons learned from the crash in the late 1980s. Experts have been predicting a market crash and correction ever since the average house price has exceeded average income. However, the problem with this scenario is that it hasn't yet happened and that's probably because it does not take into account the many differences in the housing market and economic conditions between now and the late 1980s (see box opposite).

must know

What causes change?
The main factors affecting the UK property market are as follows:
▶ The level of first-time buyers or investors.
▶ The level of interest rates.
▶ The shortage of property stock versus the demand for property.

Property price surveys

Now it is time to start to understand how to interpret the property price survey reports that help to price properties at a local, as well as national, level. In the UK, there are many different property price surveys. In the main, these cover only England and Wales, but there are other surveys that cover Scotland and Ireland.

Make the right choice

The table opposite gives a summary of the different property surveys, how they report and when they are released to the press. It is from these press releases that the media obtain the information for their headlines.

Surveys that measure current and future house prices

Both the Rightmove and Hometrack surveys are useful for looking at current market trends and gaining an idea of what has been happening over the previous month, as well as giving the best indication of what might happen over the next few months. Both measure the market nationally and at county level.

Rightmove is a property website (see page 38) that advertises more than 500,000 properties for sale and rent in the UK from lots of different estate agents. Their survey measures the changes in asking prices across the country and Rightmove has the biggest coverage of all of the property price surveys. However, it is important to remember that an *asking* price is not necessarily the same as the *actual* price paid for a property. If the market is moving fast, it may underestimate the final price agreed; if the market is slow, it may overestimate the market as people will place their offers below the asking price.

Hometrack (see page 38) obtains information from over 3,000 estate agents around England and Wales. The benefit of this survey

Organizations that produce property price surveys

Survey	Frequency	How they report	Issue date
Land Registry	Quarterly	Released to the press, but all information is on their own website as a pdf file	Issued one month in arrears for each quarter (January–March data issued in May)
Halifax	National: monthly Regional: quarterly	Released to the press, but all information is on their own website in an easy-to-use format	First week of every month
Nationwide	National: monthly Regional: quarterly	Released to the press, but all information is on their own website in an easy-to-use format	Last week in the month and the regional indices at the end of each quarter
Hometrack	Monthly	Released to the press, but summary information is listed on their website under 'news'. Can purchase information for your local area from their website	Last week in month
Rightmove	Monthly	Released to the press and gives information based on the asking property prices of the estate agents that advertise their properties on the Rightmove website	Monthly, usually the second week
Royal Institute of Chartered Surveyors (RICS)	Monthly	Typically by press release and a summary is listed on their own website in their 'news' section	Monthly on the third Wednesday

is that it collates information on the agreed price of a property for sale and also on the number of buyers and sellers registering with estate agents, the average number of viewings it takes to gain a sale and the time needed to complete the transaction. This can be really useful as it gives a good idea, at a local level, of the demand as well as the supply of properties, and can help you assess how long it might take to sell your property as well as estimate the price you may receive.

Surveys that measure recent activity
**The Halifax House Price Survey and the
Nationwide House Price Index** are the two main
surveys in this bracket. Both of these surveys gain their
data from their mortgage-lending business, with Halifax
having the bigger sample size of the two. The prices are
noted after the companies have sent a surveyor out to
the property to be purchased, so they measure prices
after the original offer price, which can change and
happens either within a month or eight weeks of the
offer being made.

These companies have, up until recently, led the
property price surveys and their information is really
useful to the banks and those interested in national
property price movements. Both companies offer a
facility on their websites (see page 38) to price your
house at current market value by using their 'trend' data.
All you have to do is put in the price you bought it for,
your postcode and the date that you bought the
property. However, their information relates only to
mortgaged property and does not include fully owned
properties, so the surveys can sometimes underestimate
market prices.

**The Royal Institute of Chartered Surveyors
(RICS)** also measures property prices at a similar stage
to the mortgage companies and they have over 350
surveyors, some of whom are also estate agents. The
benefit of their survey (see page 38) is that it also takes
into account the condition of the property, rather than
being based on the original offer price, which can often
be reduced if an adverse survey report is received.

**The Survey of Mortgage Lenders by the Office
of the Deputy Prime Minister** is a relatively new
monthly survey (see page 38) that was launched in

September 2003. It has been taking data from 50 mortgage lenders, noting approximately 25,000 completions per month. It bases the property price data on the final paid price, after any renegotiation stage. The data also monitors first-time buyer activity, the type of mortgage people are taking out and the number of repossessions, so it does give a good 'all round' indication of what is happening in the market as well as what is happening to property prices.

Surveys that measure the market quarterly

The Land Registry provides the most accurate measure of what is happening in the property market, as it includes all transactions for a quarter. Unfortunately, as the information is collated quarterly and released one month after the end of each quarter, it may be out of date if the market is going rapidly up or down and it therefore may not help you to price your own property. Also the data is provided for broad groups of properties: Detached, Semi-detached, Terraced and Flats. It doesn't allow you to narrow down the prices to a specific type of property, such as a three-bed semi, but gives an average price for each group.

What the Land Registry can be useful for is checking to see how many properties are being sold in your area, and you can match other surveys to this history to gain a fuller picture of price movements over a six to 12-month period.

Media reports and property price surveys

Where property is concerned, the media are very much prone to making dramatic announcements and producing eye-catching headlines. From 1999, as we have already seen on page 14, property prices have in

good to know

National not local reporting
Another issue regarding media coverage of property price surveys is that the prices quoted tend to be for property nationwide or, at best, within large regional areas. What the press rarely does is look at individual property markets, such as the market for older properties, properties requiring renovation, local property markets, or the pricing of newly built versus second-hand homes.

A better source of information on your local property market is more likely to be the regional property paper or supplement, particularly one that quotes the region's statistics and then regularly interviews local estate agents for updates of what is happening within a specific area.

fact grown successively month on month, quarter on quarter, with nothing more calamitous than the odd 'dip'.

Reports on the property market in 2003: The last property price dip that took place was in March 2003, after which property surveys reported a slowdown in the increase in property prices and market activity. The media immediately led with titles such as 'property price crash imminent'. The result was that buyers, having previously witnessed rapidly rising prices, felt they now had time to make an offer and look at every property they wanted to, rather than offering on a property 'under pressure' with house prices rising. They held off making offers just in case prices really were coming down.

What followed was a self-fulfilling prophecy. As buyers held back from making offers, sellers who needed to secure a sale started to reduce their prices to encourage buyers to make an offer. Prices began to dip and sales started to slide. The property surveys then reported that 'prices have continued to slow' and that now buyers were holding off. Not all sellers reduced their prices, however, so some properties remained on the market. Some vendors decided to withdraw their properties from sale as it was so quiet and other people who had been thinking about selling were losing confidence in the market and consequently didn't put their property up for sale.

By the summer of 2003, buyers had seen all the properties available and sellers were being more realistic about their prices, so sales started to be made. The stock had been reduced back down to the level of demand. The property surveys then started to talk of increased sales and numbers of buyers. More people began to come back into the market and, as most areas were still short of property stock, confidence in the market was regained and prices started to go up again.

The property market in 2004: Even in the latter part of 2004, when monthly and quarterly property price surveys continued to report doom and gloom, the upshot was that rather than property prices in 2004 being less than those in 2003, as might be anticipated, prices still increased nationally between 10 and 15%. There were, however, dramatic regional differences. Some areas around London and the Home Counties, for example, hardly grew at all and some places fell slightly, while Wales grew by over 20%.

What influences house prices nationally and locally

Property prices can vary just on one street, whether they are 1930s semis, a whole street of Victorian terraces or a road of properties from different periods. So using national guidelines can rarely help you to price your own property, it can only give a guide to property buying/selling market conditions.

Get hold of information

What you need to know are the main factors affecting house prices at a national and local level. Using this information, with the help of the price surveys and your own local knowledge, you can then work out what is happening in your own property market and estimate the price of your property and the one you are buying.

What causes house prices to rise nationally

There are many factors that affect house prices over and above the media and property price surveys. The ones that affect prices on a national level tend to relate to economic conditions and general supply and demand for property.

   Economic conditions: Our ability to afford a home is determined by three key factors:

▶ Employment levels.

▶ Level of disposable income.

▶ Percentage of income taken by mortgage repayments.

   All of these 'affordability' factors affect the level of confidence people have when buying and selling a home. If you are concerned about losing your job, for instance, and your salary is not increasing, then you are less likely to risk selling your own home to buy a bigger version or one in a better location.

Apart from job security, the level of interest rates directly affects the property market. Interest rates determine, for most people, the amount of mortgage they pay each month. Unless your mortgage is on a fixed interest or capped rate, an increase in the interest rates by the Bank of England will be followed within a few weeks or months by a letter from your mortgage lender advising you of the increased cost of your mortgage.

Hometrack calculate that, in the UK, due to mortgages being based on affordability as opposed to income multiples, for interest rate rises really to affect people's ability to afford their mortgage repayments they would have to rise above 7%. At this level, people will be less likely to move, dampening down the demand and number of properties on the market. Under these circumstances, only properties that are realistically priced will sell.

Supply and demand: Another factor that affects house price movement over and above affordability is the demand for properties – which also relies on the 'confidence' of people to buy and the supply of property, which, as we have seen, is under pressure because not enough suitable properties, especially small ones, are being built in the right areas to cater for the increased demand.

What causes house prices to rise locally

Factors affecting the local, as opposed to national, housing market are much more varied. To get to grips with your own local property market, it is worth spending some time picking a property type, preferably one different from the one you are hoping to sell. For example, you could look at three-bedroom semis or two-bedroom flats in the area. Then get hold of your local weekly property paper and jot down how many are for sale, maximum and minimum prices and any price changes over a number of weeks.

Once you have done this, then try to work out why some are more expensive than others. For example, a two-bed flat in a Victorian building might be more expensive than comparable accommodation in a 1960s block. A top-floor flat might be more

1 How to value a property

must know

Main factors affecting property prices locally

- Increased investment in the area.
- Ease of access to road, rail and airport.
- Local amenities.
- Local job market.
- Changes in the local population.
- School results.
- Crime rates.
- Busy roads, railway lines, other noise disturbances.
- Pylons and electrical sub-stations.
- Property type (age, character, fashion for purchasing a particular type of property).

expensive than a ground-floor one. Flats with garages or parking spaces might differ in price, too.

On top of this, it is critical to ascertain what is happening in your local area that might influence prices in specific parts of the area you are buying and selling in (see box left). This is particularly true if you are looking for a property to be an investment, as opposed to your own permanent home.

Increased investment in the area: If an area has a new company moving in, or is attracting people to move there because of its amenities (such as a local airport offering cheap flights), then the population will increase and property prices are likely to rise. As people move from other areas around the country, then those areas may decline. Nationally this might be reported as 'no change' in house prices, but regionally one area will see an increase in property prices while another may see prices fall.

School results: These are now having an enormous impact on property prices and RICS estimates that people will pay up to a 12% premium to be in the catchment area of a good school. This is an important point to bear in mind, for if you are looking to sell your property in an area where the schools are not so good, you may have to pay more for exactly the same property only a few streets away, but in a better catchment area.

Property type: In addition to all these factors, the individual characteristics of the property itself need to be borne in mind as they will affect the price you get for your property and consequently what you can pay for the one you want to buy (see box right). For example, a property on a centrally located tree-lined street of three- and four-bedroom Victorian houses in the catchment area of a good school is likely to cost more than a new build of a similar size on an out-of-town estate.

Getting a better price for your house

The key to maximizing your property's value is to make it the most desirable property of its type for sale within your locality, as most people who buy and sell property move locally, usually within a five-mile radius.

First, it is essential to consult the internet and/or your local property paper to find out the maximum you could get for your property. Once you have an idea of the potential price of your property, you can then investigate ways of trying to increase its value based on your research of what similar properties have and on studying the latest fashions in interior and exterior décor. However, there are some basic rules that every seller must try to adhere to, without which it may be difficult to persuade people to pay the maximum amount.

The key features that most properties need to show are:

▶ A balance of accommodation (see box overleaf).
▶ Tidying, de-cluttering and de-personalizing the property (by removing family photos and other memorabilia, for instance).
▶ Making sure it appeals to a broad market – to a young family, for instance, as well as a more mature couple.
▶ Spruce up the exterior of the house with container plants and a well-kept drive and manicured garden.

must know

Characteristics of a property that affect its price
▶ Size of the property – number of bedrooms, reception rooms.
▶ Having a garden, or the size of the plot.
▶ Parking facilities from on street to allotted bays, permits and a garage.
▶ Condition of the property and what work needs doing.
▶ Character of the property.
▶ Age of the property.

---

must know

Deciding on the price

▶ Having a property with a good 'balance' means that the amount of living accommodation should be in proportion to the number of bedrooms and size of garden or parking space. For example, it is difficult to sell a family-sized five-bedroom house when there is no or little garden or anywhere to park the car close by. If you have three reception rooms and large spaces downstairs, but only two small bedrooms upstairs, this limits the market – and price – you can get for your property.

▶ Every property has a maximum price that someone will pay for it. Up until recently, it has been very difficult to establish the 'maximum' price that might be obtained for properties along a particular road or within a certain area. This is now much easier as the Land Registry are licensing their data to the private sector, who either provide this information for free or for a small charge per property.

▶ To find out how much people paid for properties in your street or the one you are hoping to buy in, there are certain websites you can check (see page 38).

▶ Try to keep the interior in line with fashion – such as adding an en-suite shower room, study or creating a breakfast diner.

Buying property as an investment

Looking to buy a property as an investment rather than somewhere to live is a much more difficult task. The crucial point about buying to invest is not necessarily to invest in a property that you personally like, but to identify what will provide the best investment return.

Old versus new: You may love old houses, but if you are hoping to rent the property out, then you need to remember that old buildings tend to be more expensive to maintain. By contrast, sellers of 'new builds' may offer excellent incentives such as guaranteed income schemes, payment of stamp duty or purchase fees, and this may give you a much better return in the long run than a property you prefer personally.

Predicting where best to buy: You also need to decide whether you want to invest for the long term as a buy to let or for the short term as a renovation project or building from scratch on a plot of land you have purchased. Whatever you decide, you need to investigate the market thoroughly. It is worth checking local government websites to see what changes they are making. For example, the new M6 toll road may mean easier access and commuting from areas further afield, and cheaper properties in the area may increase in value. It may simply be that a better train service is being offered, or a new tram link added. If you can find out this information before it becomes public knowledge there is a good chance that if you purchase a property early enough you will see a better return on your investment over time.

However, this can be a relatively risky option to take, as you have to decide whether to invest in a property prior to a decision being made by the local council or after the decision when prices may already have risen to reflect better transport links to the area. It can also take years for the plans to take effect, so you must be willing to invest for years, not months.

Talking to the experts: Another very effective approach is to talk to all the local estate agents or visit the local branch of RICS to find out which places are seeing an increase in prices or buyer interest. It may even be that the local paper reports that a currently poorly rated school has just appointed a new head teacher who has turned around other schools or come from a school with a good reputation. If the school's performance looks likely to improve, property prices will almost certainly rise.

Professional property valuations

Apart from checking for yourself the price of your own property or the property you are looking to buy, the property professionals can also help. However, it is important not to rely entirely on their valuations.

Research the market

If you take time to research the market yourself, you will often gain a picture as good as that of the professionals. What this knowledge also gives you is an ability to tell whether the property professional really knows their stuff or not!

The second reason why it is important to know how the professionals value property is because an agreed offer price should always be subject to a confirmed mortgage offer on the property or to the findings of your own survey. The mortgage lender wants to confirm that the property is worth what you have offered for it before they agree to lend their money. The surveyor's report of the property's condition is also important and may mean you alter your original offer.

How estate agents value a property

Estate agents generally operate within a fairly small area. Some may cover only a few miles within cities or towns, while others in more rural areas may cover a patch of up to 20 or 30 miles. Based on information gained from their own business (see box left), they know better than anyone else what a property can be 'marketed' for and what level of price they think you should achieve for the property.

Good agents: A good agent will also keep an eye on what is happening locally so that they better understand how

good to know

The information estate agents can provide
▶ How many buyers they have on their books.
▶ A list of what type of properties buyers are looking for.
▶ What properties are currently for sale and those coming onto the market.
▶ What price properties have sold for.
▶ The physical differences between similar properties.

prices may be affected in the future. Any estate agent worth working with will come to your house to make a free valuation or marketing appraisal. They should bring with them a selection of properties that they have sold in the last 3–6 months that are similar to yours and give you an idea of:

▶ How long they were on the market for.
▶ How much they have sold for .

They should then go around your property with you, comparing your property with others they have sold or currently have up for sale, and only then will they be able to suggest an appropriate asking price. However, no agent should give just one price. They should always offer:

▶ A suggested asking or marketing price.
▶ A price to accept if offered below this.
▶ A price for a quick sale (to achieve a sale within six weeks).

What they will not do is take into account any structural problems that might reduce the final property value or items not immediately visible, such as damp, subsidence or leaking roofs.

An accurate valuation: Agents know that many people selling their home will give their business to the agent that quotes a higher price than their rivals. Some agents do this in the hope that you will place your property with their agency, and when no offers have come forward, they will suggest you reduce the price. Others, who may be commissioned to get quick sales for the business, may do exactly the opposite. Some agents may also not have much experience in selling properties like yours, so having only a few or no comparables may mean the price is wrong from the start.

The best way to assess which agents are giving the most accurate price is to ask a minimum of three agents to make a valuation. It may even be helpful to have four or five agents to value the property, particularly if the first three give you a price range wider than a 5% difference.

Local knowledge: It is important to question the agents when they visit, especially on the number of buyers they have on their books, whether they are local or from outside the area and how many are looking to buy your type of property or within your price range. It is also important to work with an agent who can show that they sell properties like yours locally and have examples for you to see.

How a mortgage lender values a property

A mortgage lender values your property for a very different reason to an estate agent. They also use different methods of valuation and take into account different factors when deciding whether they should risk lending you the money – or not. The reason a mortgage lender values a property is to verify that if you default on the payment and the property gets repossessed, they can recoup the money they lent you.

Mortgage lender's survey: Unlike the estate agent, who offers a free valuation, most mortgage lenders charge for theirs, even though it is for their own purposes. They may use their own trained valuers or surveying practice, if they own one. Alternatively, they may just instruct a local surveyor from a panel of independent surveyors that they have negotiated special rates with. They will also check the value of other properties for which they have supplied mortgages in the past.

The valuation: What a mortgage lender's valuation does is verify that the property is accurately described in the estate agent's details. For example, if the details say that it has 'three bedrooms', that it definitely has three bedrooms, not two plus a room you couldn't get a bed into. Increasingly, mortgage lenders do provisional checks on the condition of the property, such as a check for damp on the walls and floors, plus assessing whether any renovation work needs to be done.

In some cases, if the valuer feels that essential work is required, the mortgage lender may withhold some of the money they are lending to you until the work is completed to their satisfaction. Again, they do this to protect themselves, as if you default on your mortgage payments, they don't then want to pay more for repairs. In some cases, the valuer may also decide that the property is not worth the price that you agreed and give their different valuation to

good to know

Types of fee
The mortgage valuation fee can either be a fixed fee or dependent on the price of the property you are going to buy. For example, it can be as little as a few hundred pounds to over £1,000 for properties at the top end of the market.

the mortgage lender. In response, the mortgage lender may leave you with the choice of 'topping up the difference' yourself or reducing the offer price in line with the valuer's conclusions.

Additional surveys: The time that it takes to do a mortgage valuation is about an hour, but valuers can and will, if required, recommend or insist that further specialist surveys, such as timber and damp surveys, are carried out by you, but for the benefit of themselves before they confirm their offer.

Environmental factors: Along with the valuation, the mortgage lender usually has a database of localities that need further checks carrying out. For example, if your property is in an area where there is a high risk of flooding or in a former coal-mining district, which could lead to subsidence, they may ask you (usually via your legal representative) to gain these additional reassurances that the property is not only in good order, but also constructed on solid ground. They are also likely to give an indication of how much the property would cost to rebuild. The reason they do this is that you have to insure the building as well as the contents of a property. The cost of rebuilding would not be the same as the amount you paid for it as that price includes the land as well as the building.

Instructing a surveyor of your own

The fact that the mortgage lender is conducting a valuation does not mean you do not need to instruct a surveyor of your own. On the contrary, it is extremely important that you do so as you will appoint a surveyor who is working on your behalf, not the lender's. The mortgage valuation gives you no protection against physical or environmental problems associated with your property. In fact, some surveyors that work for mortgage lenders on valuations are employed on the basis of having to do a certain number of surveys a day. As a result, they may not have the time to spend at the property doing a good check for you as well as obtaining the minimum information required by the mortgage lender.

Ideally you should instruct a surveyor from a different practice to that of the mortgage lender to ensure that you are getting more than one opinion as well as independent professional advice.

How a surveyor values a property

A surveyor has to be professionally qualified and, in the UK, will usually belong to the Royal Institute of Chartered Surveyors. Having an independent survey on your property is as important as getting a proper inspection done on a second-hand car before buying it. If the survey identifies previously unknown problems, the money you spent on getting the survey can be recouped by using it to renegotiate the price.

The surveyor should know the local area well and should be able to give you a guide on what type of land the property has been built

must know

Homebuyer's survey and valuation report
This report is typically 10–20 pages long, requires paying for and gives a summary of:
▶ The property's physical condition.
▶ What needs urgent attention.
▶ Any local factors that you should be aware of.
▶ A view of the property's value.

The survey checks specifically for damp and potential timber problems, or renovation work associated with roofing, insulation, guttering and other drainage, as well as giving you an idea of what it would cost to rebuild the property should anything happen to it.

This figure is always much lower than the suggested value as it takes into account that you already own the land it is to be built on. This information is crucial as you will need it to work out the level of buildings insurance you will need to take out.

Building survey
This is a much more in-depth survey of the property's structure and condition. It is generally for older or more unusual properties, listed buildings and, in particular, any properties requiring renovation. You would also need to pay for it.

It covers everything that the homebuyer's survey does, although some surveyors do not give a value for the property. Instead, they provide a list of 'works to be done' and an estimated cost of how much it will be to get them sorted.

on and what problems might occur as a result. For example, drier weather over a number of years followed by period of heavy rain can result in movement in clay-based soil, shifting buildings and causing subsidence. Other factors a surveyor should mention are any adverse local issues such as not being on a bus route or being close to a landfill site (see pages 132–3).

A further survey that you can have done is a gas and electrical survey (see page 166). This is a requirement for landlords of properties, but can help you assess whether the wiring or boiler need replacing.

Which property professional will give you the most accurate property valuation

Realistically, this has to be the surveyor's report – be it a homebuyer's survey or building report (see box opposite). A local surveyor will know the individual factors affecting your property and its condition and they should be well acquainted with the prices in your area.

It is also the only independent valuation of a property you will have. The estate agent primarily works on behalf of the seller to get the best price. As we have seen, the mortgage lender's valuation is done to cover themselves, to assess the level of risk in lending you the money. Your surveyor, on the other hand, gets paid a fixed price and there is the security of a complaints procedure if you discover any significant problems once you have purchased a property that were not identified in the survey.

In the end, however, the true value of a property is what you are willing to pay for it and what the seller is willing to sell it for.

Step-by-step guide to valuing a property
Whether you are thinking about buying, selling or investing in a property, there are steps you should take to ensure you get a good idea of what is happening both nationally and locally that might affect your purchase.

1 Understand the national market
▶ Read the Sunday property papers, such as *The Times*, *Telegraph* or *Independent*, to obtain an overview of what is happening.
▶ Check the detailed regional picture by looking at the main property price reports (see table on page 19).

2 Understand your local market
▶ Read your local property paper supplement for market comment and any new local developments.
▶ Work out your own property type and size.
▶ Track the prices and sales of similar properties in a 3–5 mile radius.
▶ Work out why some sell for more while others sell for less, some go quickly while others seem to 'stick'.
▶ Work out a maximum and minimum price you think your property will sell for.

3 Understand the market for the property you wish to sell/buy
▶ Use property websites (see pages 18–19) to see how many properties there are of the type you are looking to sell/buy. Do this by:
  – putting in your postcode
  – searching within a radius of 3–5 miles
  – inserting your maximum and minimum price
  – putting in the minimum number of bedrooms you require
  – including 'sold' or 'under offer'.
▶ Look at how many properties you will be competing with/for.

4 Speak to estate agents locally
▶ If instructing to sell, contact at least three estate agents and ask them to value your property (see pages 30–1). Request:

- asking price
- achievable price
- price for a quick sale.

▶ If wanting to buy:
- contact all your local estate agents
- give them your minimum requirements
- give them a maximum and minimum price you would pay
- ask them for the best locations or the locations that would give you best value for money.

5 Find out how much similar properties have gone for on your road

▶ If you know that properties near yours have sold within the past 3–6 months, check what price they sold for using the property survey websites (see page 18–19).

▶ If you know what they sold for six months ago and the property price surveys say the market has gone up or down by 6% since then, apply this to the properties' sold prices.

▶ If your property is very different to others up and down the road, do not forget that there will be a maximum that you will receive for it as every road has its own 'ceiling' price.

6 Allow for the property's condition

▶ If you are selling and your property is not in good condition, or it has a value in excess of £500,000, it may be worth instructing a surveyor for a homebuyer's report (see box on page 34) as it may help you assess what work is worth doing and what you could leave to the buyer, and discount from the price accordingly.

▶ If you are buying, always have a homebuyer's survey as a minimum check on the property's value.

7 Obtain quotes for all renovation work

▶ If the survey highlights more work that needs to be done to the property, obtain three quotes from builders or specialists before you finalize your offer.

want to know more?

Property price surveys

For England and Wales
Halifax House Price Index
tel. 0870 600 5000
www.hbosplc.com/economy/
housingresearch.asp

Hometrack
tel. 0800 019 4440
www.hometrack.co.uk

Land Registry
tel. 0151 473 6137
www.landreg.gov.uk/propertyprice/

Nationwide House Price Index
www.nationwide.co.uk/hpi/

Rightmove
www.rightmove.co.uk

Royal Institute of Chartered Surveyors (RICS)
Housing Market Survey
tel. 0870 333 1600
www.rics.org.uk/Property/Residentialproperty/
Residentialpropertymarket/

Office of the Deputy Prime Minister
tel. 020 7944 4400
www.odpm.gov.uk

TEAM is a group of estate agents that work as a
national network and produce their own
property price survey:
tel. 0870 848 8848 / 0700 560 7216
www.teamprop.co.uk/articles.asp

Outside England and Wales
Halifax and Nationwide also cover Scotland and
Northern Ireland. RICS and TEAM also cover
Scotland.

Houseprice Scotland gives you house price
information from across Scotland:
tel. 0113 228 4452
www.housepricescotland.com

The University of Ulster produces its own survey:
tel. 028 9036 6178
www.ulster.ac.uk/news/releases

Regional price information
This website, which mainly covers the
Southeast, offers very good 'asking price'
information. You have to search for a property
within a specific area to obtain information on it:
www.findaproperty.co.uk

Estate agents' property price index
The website of the National Association of
Estate Agents (NAEA) gives information
obtained from their nationwide property
database. Contact:
tel. 01926 496800
www.naea.co.uk

Information on previous property sales
Recently, the information has been licensed
from government sources and has been made
available on the internet. Some companies
charge per property, per month or per postcode,
while others have decided to allow you to gain
the information for free – as long as you give
them your details in return:
www.housepricecrash.com
www.landregisteronline.gov.uk
www.mouseprice.com
www.myhouseprice.com

Buying property as an investment

There are many property investment sites and there is much training information on the internet, but many organizations are simply after your money rather than offering you good, impartial advice.

The Property Secrets website is a 'club' for investors and shares lots of information. You do need to subscribe for some sections, but if you are serious about investing it should be helpful: www.propertysecrets.net

The best sources of information to consult when looking to buy a property for investment are:

▶ Local newspapers
▶ Local estate agents
▶ Local council websites and planning departments.

Gas and electrical surveys

For more information, visit:
www.gas-elec.co.uk

Trade shows

These can be really helpful when it comes to buying and selling a home and especially when you are looking to invest. They often run useful seminars and introduce you to new products and services that are on the market. For more details, see page 189 or contact Homebuyer Events:
tel. 020 8877 3636
www.homebuyerevents.co.uk

Additional sources of information

▶ National newspapers – particularly their weekend property reports, usually appearing on a Sunday.
▶ Local newspapers – these usually have a special property supplement on Wednesdays, Thursdays or Fridays.
▶ Local estate agents – talk to your local estate agent about current trends.

Other housing statistics

If you are keen to find out more facts and figures connected with the housing market, then these organizations offer lots of useful statistics:

Council of Mortgage Lenders
tel. 020 7437 0075
www.cml.org.uk

Office of the Deputy Prime Minister
tel. 020 7944 4400
www.odpm.gov.uk

Office of National Statistics
tel. 0845 601 3034
www.statistics.gov.uk

2 How to choose the right services

To buy and sell a property you can enlist the help of at least ten different services – or you can choose to do it yourself. Based on the sale and purchase of a £150,000 property, the cost of using these services amounts to nearly four times the cost of doing it yourself. On the surface, the DIY option may seem a good idea, but it can be extremely time-consuming and with hidden pitfalls, with the result that most movers tend to choose to use the professionals instead. So what services do you need and which should you choose?

How the service providers can help

Choosing the right services to help you move can make all the difference when buying/selling a property. It can also take the stress out of this 'minefield' of a process. The charts opposite will give an idea of when you should organize and book the services that you need.

Buying in theory and practice

The theory of buying and selling a home is simple. The practice, however, is much more complicated. This is because each purchase and sale is different, according to the current laws that apply, the condition and type of property and your own circumstances.

For example, if you are considering buying a property to renovate it, you need to bear in mind that any new building has to adhere to building regulations and planning rules. There can be rights of way to consider, in addition to local issues, such as conservation or redevelopment, that can determine the extent to which you may alter a property or add to its future value. Recently, new regulations have come into force that require you to fill in forms showing where you have obtained the finances to purchase the property and what type of property you have bought. Soon even more regulations will be coming into play that will change the way your property is marketed in the future.

Buying a property

What you need to do	Mortgage agreement in principle	Finding a property	Making an offer	Accepting an offer	Exchanging contracts	Completion
Instruct/ call/ search for:	Independent financial adviser (IFA) Mortgage lender Mortgage broker	Buying agent Estate agents' mailing lists Local property paper/ supplements Internet Solicitor/ conveyancer quotes	Solicitor/ conveyancer Surveyor quotes	Survey of the property Confirm mortgage lender/ broker/IFA mortgage offer Removal quotes Storage quotes	Confirm buildings insurance Confirm removals/ storage Prepare change of address	Confirm contents insurance Finalize change of address Organize cleaner

Selling a property

What you need to do	Property for sale	Accepting an offer	Exchanging contracts	Completing contracts
Instruct/ call/ search for:	Estate agent/ auction house Home-staging company Cleaner Storage company Solicitor/ conveyancer quotes	Solicitor/ conveyancer Removal/storage quotes	Confirm removals/storage Prepare change of address Advise utility companies Book meter readings	Finalize change of address Organize cleaner

Doing it yourself

It is possible to do all this yourself, but it does need a high level of expertise and attention to detail and will take up several hours per week. So it is important to weigh up the difficulty of the task, degree of expertise and time it will take, versus the cost of paying for someone else to do the work. The table below is a rough guide and shows that the whole process – excluding searching for or visiting properties – can take over 100 hours! It is also not possible to act on behalf of your own mortgage when it comes to the legal side of things, the one aspect of conveyancing you can't do yourself, so you will have to instruct a legal firm to do this for you.

Summary of services

Service	Level of expertise	Example time taken (in hours)	Estimated service cost
Estate agent	3 out of 5	24	1–4% of sale of the property
Mortage	3 out of 5	16	£0 to several £1,000s
Conveyancing	4 out of 5	24	£450 plus
Property survey	5 out of 5	8	£400 plus
Insurance	2 out of 5	8	£0 to several £100s
Removal	2 out of 5	24	£500 plus

Note: Costs vary according to the size and contents of a property.

Criticism of the service providers

When buying a home, there is often much criticism of service providers by those involved in the process, which is reflected by reports in the media. It is easy to feel that the agent is just after their commission, the mortgage lender is trying to 'trap you' or the surveyor is colluding with the estate agent or lender. Realistically, this does not happen often, but due to the lack of regulation in some areas and the poor reputation attributed to some of these services, it is easy to feel that there is nothing to choose between them, that the cheapest or quickest service offered is the best one to take. Unfortunately, this can compound the problem, as a cheap service often translates into a poor one. For a successful move, good professional help and support can be well worth paying for. The trick is to know how to find it.

---

must know

New regulations
Rules for buying and selling a property will be coming in, especially with regard to England and Wales, which will change the way we buy and sell property in the future, and it is important to keep an eye on when these new rules will be implemented and understand what they are.

Choosing an estate agent

To sell a property at the best price, to the best buyer, taking into account the seller's position, you need an estate agent. Estate agents are not yet regulated in the UK, so they can decide for themselves the best methods of selling a property.

Legal requirements

There are legal requirements set out in the Estate Agency Act of 1979 and the Property Misdescriptions Act of 1991 that estate agents have to adhere to. But most agents will offer and perform certain basic tasks (see box opposite).

However, many estate agents offer more help during the buying and selling process, while some companies voluntarily adhere to codes of practice or are members of associations and schemes (see page 80) that offer a guarantee of good service, whether you are a buyer or a seller.

Around one in every three sales falls through after the offer stage, many coming unstuck due to problems that simply needed a bit more attention to detail to pre-empt/solve them. A full understanding of the buying and selling process will help to resolve any issues that arise, to keep the sale or purchase moving forward. A good agent will anticipate and help solve these problems.

Valuation visit

During the initial visit to value your property, a good agent should:

▶ Give a good overview of what is happening in the local market.
▶ Advise on what changes you should make to your property to help it sell.
▶ Discuss with you:
    – what time-frame you want to sell in at the price that you need to achieve.
    – what you are looking to buy next.
▶ Offer an asking price, one that is achievable and a price for a quick sale.
▶ Talk you through their terms and conditions, especially discussing the price and length of time you are contracted to them for.
▶ Give an indication of the number of buyers they have looking at your property type and price range.

Basic tasks of an estate agent selling a property
- Making an initial visit to your property to value it.
- Giving examples of similar property recently sold in your road/area.
- Indicating how much they think your property is worth.
- Producing sales particulars of your property by taking photos inside/out, taking measurements of all rooms, agreeing what is to be left at the property.
- Sending you the sales particulars for your authorization.
- Issuing you with their terms and conditions of business.
- Advertising your property in the local newspapers, their window, on the internet and to a list of buyers.
- Putting a board up outside your property.
- Organizing and booking viewings for buyers.
- Receiving offers and passing on in writing any offers they receive.
- Sending a letter if an offer is accepted, including conditions of sale to the seller, the buyer and the seller's and buyer's solicitors.
- Coordinating the handover of keys on completion/moving day.

Basic tasks of an estate agent buying a property
- Taking down the details of the type of property you are looking for, including areas that you are interested in, the price rang, the number of rooms and any other requirements (e.g. garden, garage).
- Adding you to their mailing list.
- Organizing any viewings.
- Calling you with any new instructions that fit your requirements.
- Discussing and receiving any offers you put forward in writing to the vendor.

Managing the sale

A good estate agent will make the effort to 'manage the change' or sales progression for both buyers and sellers. What this means is they will make all the necessary phone calls to:
- The buyer/seller.
- The buyer's and seller's conveyancers.
- Other estate agents involved in the chain.
- The financial companies.
- The surveyor.

If they are very organized, they will give you a set time for a weekly update on what is happening. Some companies have specialist 'sales progression' staff or departments, or just a conscientious employee who regards it as part of their job to see the sale right through to completion.

Managing property visits

A good estate agent should provide an accurate picture of the buyer's ability to purchase by checking:

▶ Their financial situation.

▶ Whether they have a mortgage agreement in principle.

▶ The status of their property sale if relevant.

▶ How interested they are in buying a particular property.

▶ How quickly they want to move.

Managing the offer

If an offer is made, a good estate should:

▶ Give a balanced view on whether to accept the offer or not.

▶ Know the buyer's financial position/ability to purchase.

▶ Make sure you agree what is in/not in the sale (e.g. carpets and curtains).

Many good agents will also make the effort to produce a booklet or helpful sheets on the buying and selling process and what assistance they give from start to finish of the process, in addition to a complaints procedure if you are unhappy with their service.

did you know?

You must provide accurate information

The agent is reliant on you for the information they put in their sales particulars, such as length of leasehold or what is included/excluded in the sale. You must therefore make sure this information is accurate before giving it to them as it affects the buyer's rights under the Property Misdescriptions Act of 1991.

Different types of estate agent

Just as each agent offers a different service, so each is owned and run in different ways. Understanding the different types of estate agent will help you to know what to expect when dealing with them, which may affect which agent you choose.

All estate agents usually have a similar personnel structure:

Estate agency manager

Senior negotiator

Negotiator

Administrative assistant

Estate agents typically earn a small basic salary, but earn a commission on property they sell or the 'lead' they generate for other services such as conveyancing, mortgage lending or insurance. This level of commission depends on how the company is structured. Other staff that can either be recruited by the estate agency or affiliated to are:

▶ Chartered surveyors
▶ Independent financial advisers (IFAs) or mortgage brokers
▶ Solicitors/licensed conveyancers.

Nationwide coverage: Estate agents offering a national coverage are usually owned by financial institutions, a few large estate agent groups or gain national coverage from affiliating themselves with marketing networks. The financial institutions hope to gain mortgages, insurance and conveyancing business from buyers and sellers. The largest estate agency group is Countrywide, who operate under many different company names and are one of the few estate agency listed on the stock market. For an estate agent to belong to an affiliation network, they usually pay for the privilege. This buys national coverage through centrally produced magazines and internet sites.

Associated services: Because of these affiliations and methods of reward for the agency, it is likely that staff will ask you if you have already organized your mortgage or surveyor/solicitor. Some companies are even willing to reduce their selling fee if you take their services. Before you choose any of their services, however, you should check them out thoroughly, comparing them with those offered by other companies.

Do remember, however, that some agents will insist that buyers be 'checked out' to make sure they have enough funds to purchase at the level they are looking at and are 'serious buyers'. If you are not keen to use the estate agent's services then it is better to organize them yourself first and let the agent have the details so there is no need for any other referrals.

Finally, corporate or large offices can pass on your details to their other offices to contact you. In the main, this is helpful, but it is important to clarify if you want this to happen or not. It is best to have this confirmed in writing.

An estate agent's terms and conditions

These terms and conditions should adhere to contract law and to the Property Misdescriptions Act of 1991 as well as the Estate Agency Act of 1979. Most of the terms and conditions will be standard in nature, but, when you are reading through the contract, it is important that you take particular note of certain points (see box below).

Estate agent charges

Each agent will have their own series of charges for their services and their own terms and conditions of engagement for selling a property. The estate agency market is highly competitive when it comes to selling property, so they will often negotiate below their 'quoted' fees.

Sole agency: You pay lower fees by working with an estate agent on a 'sole agency' basis. This means that you agree to sell your property solely through this agent and no one else. Typically, this is for a set period of time, from a few weeks' notice to up to 26 weeks. Ideally, you would not want to sign up for more than 6–12 weeks. Sole agency charges are 1–2% of the final sale price of the property. For properties over £500,000, you can pay up to 4% commission and may have to pay for brochures or advertising in key magazines/newspapers.

Joint agency: If, for example, you wanted to sell your property quickly, or you were on the 'border' of a particular area, you might wish to look at working on a 'joint agency' basis. This can cost more as both agents do the work for free initially and each agent has less chance of selling the property (as the other may do so); hence the charge for this is 1.5–2.5%.

---

watch out!

Marketing and advertising
Make sure the terms and conditions set out what you have agreed, such as:
▶ Asking/marketing price.
▶ Contents of the sales particulars.
▶ Whether viewings are accompanied or not.
▶ How/when/where your property will be advertised.

Types of agency agreement
▶ Sole or joint.
▶ When you have to pay.
▶ How much you have to pay.

Lock-in clauses
▶ A lock-in clause is an agreement between you and the estate agent of how long you give them to market your property until you can call in another estate agency.

Estate agent checklist

- Do they sell:
  - the type of property you are looking for?
  - properties similar to the one you are selling?
- Do they answer the phone within five rings when you call?
- Do they always have someone manning the office
  - in the evening?
  - on Saturdays/Sundays?
- What are their opening/closing times, and do they suit you?
- Are they on time for valuing your property?
- Do they suggest what to do to gain the maximum price for your property?
- Do they discuss marketing and achievable prices?
- How many buyers have they looking
  - for your type of property?
  - within your price range?
- Have they sold many properties like yours within the last six months?
- If so, how many?
- How long did they take to gain an offer/sell?
- Are they a member of any organization:
  - NAEA?
  - Ombudsman Scheme?
  - Royal Institute of Chartered Surveyors (RICS)?
- What qualifications do they have?
- What training do all staff receive?
- How long have their staff worked for them?
- Do they adhere to a code of conduct, and can you have a copy?
- What is their complaints procedure?
- Will they advertise your property and for how long
  - in their window?
  - in the local property paper?
  - on the internet?
  - in other magazines/newspapers?
- What are their charges for:
  - sole agency?
  - joint agency?
- What are their terms and conditions?
  - Do you have to sign for a minimum period?
  - How long is this?
- In order to progress your sale will they talk to all of the chain (other estate agents, solicitors, etc.)?

Choosing a mortgage company

There are thousands of mortgage lenders, IFAs and mortgage brokers in the UK. Over 60% of properties bought in the UK are bought with the help of a mortgage, and the role of the mortgage lender/broker is to make sure that they sell you a mortgage that best suits your financial circumstances.

New FSA regulations

The sale and mortgage application process was not regulated by the Financial Services Authority (FSA) – unlike many other financial products and services – until October 2004. Since regulations came into force, only registered companies who have applied to the FSA for approval can sell you a mortgage. When selling you a mortgage or explaining how it works, companies must now provide you with very clear information on the charges relating to the mortgage, the way in which the mortgage repayments are calculated and the interest – or APR – you will be charged over time. It should now be easier for you to compare one mortgage with another, not be confused by complicated terminology and be clear about all charges, thus helping you to choose the right company and mortgage. Companies will be subject to investigation by the FSA if it feels that good practice is not being adhered to.

A mortgage company

The mortgage company's job is to offer you the additional money that you need to buy a property over and above any deposit you have paid.

---

good to know

Checking procedures and benefits
Before making a mortgage agreement in principle offer, lenders must:
- Assess your annual and monthly income/salary.
- Include commission earnings/bonuses.
- Assess your annual/monthly outgoings.
- Run credit checks to ensure you repay any debts you may incur.

The benefits are that:
- You do not need to have found a property to be clear about how much you will be allowed to borrow.
- It shows the estate agent that you are a serious buyer and that you can afford the property that you are interested in.
- It highlights early any issues that might prevent you receiving the mortgage offer of your choice.

To do this, each company would provisionally offer you a 'mortgage agreement in principle' giving a provisional offer of a mortgage, subject to finding a property. To make such an offer they would need to go through various checking procedures, which have a number of benefits (see box opposite). In addition, they must:

▶ Recommend the best mortgage package for you.
▶ Explain how each mortgage they suggest works.
▶ Agree with you how long you want to repay your loan for.
▶ Give a detailed breakdown of the cost of the mortgage.
▶ Put the mortgage agreement in principle in writing in a letter to you.

Once you have found a property, the mortgage company would confirm their agreement in principle with a formal offer. Basically, the company you have chosen would go through a similar process as for the offer in principle, but they repeat their initial checks and then carry out further checks, as follows:

▶ Confirm your earnings.
▶ Write to your employer.
▶ Request accounts if you are self-employed.
▶ Confirm the details of the property you are purchasing, including:
  – agent's contact details
  – full address of the property to be purchased
  – agreed purchase price.
▶ Carry out a mortgage valuation on the property.
▶ Check the value of the property versus similar properties they have offered on.
▶ Check for environmental factors that might present a risk, such as potential for subsidence or flooding.
▶ Liaise with your conveyancer for further information such as leasehold or freehold details.
▶ Send out a letter confirming their offer.
▶ Set up a direct debit from your bank account for the mortgage repayments.
▶ Release the funds to deposit the agreed mortgage finance into your solicitor's bank account.
▶ Send out a letter confirming:
  – the date each month for the mortgage repayment
  – the amount of the first and subsequent mortgage repayments.

As the market is now regulated, there should be fewer differences between companies in the way they operate and levels of efficiency. You should, however, still ask a mortgage company how quickly and efficiently they can process your application, make a formal offer and release the required funds.

Different types of mortgage companies and service costs
As with estate agents, there are different ways of finding the best mortgage for you. There are basically three types of business that can sell you a mortgage. These are:
▶ Mortgage lenders
▶ Mortgage brokers
▶ Independent financial advisers (IFAs).

Mortgage lenders will usually action your choice of mortgage at no extra cost. However, some may require you to pay an 'application fee', especially for low- or fixed-rate mortgages. This fee can vary from £100 to over £500. The downside of going to individual lenders is that you have to compare the cost of different mortgages yourself, which can take some time. Examples of mortgage lenders are Halifax and the Nationwide Building Society.

Mortgage brokers generally have access to thousands of different lenders and, in some cases, to mortgages that you will not find on the open market. They can search for the mortgage deal that best suits your financial circumstances. You need to bear in mind, however, that brokers make their money from charging you a fee to book the mortgage for you. This fee can quickly add up and can be as high as 1.5% of the mortgage, which works out at £2,250 for a £150,000 mortgage! Some will add this onto the loan, but you

must know

Mortgage lenders
▶ Bear in mind that, while a mortgage valuation may be paid for by you, it is purely for the benefit of the lender. You should never rely on the results of a mortgage valuation, and always have your own independent survey.
▶ Drawing down title deeds from a mortgage lender is required for the solicitor/legal company to sell your home. Some companies do this within days, others can take up to six weeks and this can seriously affect the time it takes to sell your home. So before you sell your property, check just how long it will take for the deeds to be drawn down.

Mortgage company checklist
- Have they been approved by the FSA to sell mortgages?
- What qualifications do they have?
- Do they adhere to a code of conduct?
- What happens if you want to complain?
- Do they check your income/expenditure?
- Have your future financial needs been assessed?
- Do they clearly lay out all the mortgage costs, including:
  - any fees for organizing the mortgage?
  - application cost?
  - mortgage valuation?
  - any early redemption penalties?
  - other fees?
- Do they explain the type of mortgage clearly, including:
  - monthly repayments?
  - how much interest you pay?
  - total repayment of the loan?
  - date for mortgage to be paid off?
  - any penalties/tie-in clauses?
- Will they help you fill in the mortgage application form?
- What commission do they gain from you taking out the mortgage with them?

need to weigh this up with the cost of obtaining a mortgage from a provider who does not charge for arranging the loan.

Independent financial advisers (IFAs) work in two different ways. They either gain a commission, referred to as a 'procurement fee', from the lender for introducing your business, or charge per hour for their services. The commission can range from 0.2% to 0.3% of the mortgage and charges can be around £75 per hour plus VAT. Bearing in mind that it can take 6–8 hours to find and sort out the right mortgage for you, charges can soon add up. In addition, IFAs charging per hour will often take the commission they would normally earn off their final fee.

Whichever service you choose, make sure that the company you go with is known to be quick and efficient and that you understand any charges you will have to pay, which will either be added to your mortgage or paid up front.

Choosing a legal firm/individual for conveyancing

A conveyancer – whether a solicitor or licensed conveyancer – is appointed to draw up contracts to transfer the title of ownership from seller to buyer. Such a person is tasked with finding any legal points that could affect the price of the property you are buying, plus handle the majority of the financial transactions.

What a conveyancer does

Conveyancing is one of the most crucial parts of the buying and selling process, and you should take time to ensure that you find and instruct a legal firm or individual that handles conveyancing (the legal process of transferring the title of a property) on a daily basis.

Any qualified solicitor can carry out conveyancing for a residential property, as it is part of their training. Because it is such

Basic legal procedures for buying/selling a property

Buying and selling	Buying only	Selling only
Verifying your identity via	Applying for searches	Creating contract of sale
▶ Passport/driving licence.	Confirming mortgage offer	Sending out property forms
▶ Three-month-old utility bill.	Passing on property forms	Drawing down deeds from mortgage lender
Exchanging contracts	Making any further enquiries on the buyer's behalf	Answering buyer's enquiries via their conveyancer
Completing contracts		
Handling all financial transactions	Advising on the contract and searches and sending the deposit to the vendor's conveyancer	Advising on the contract and receiving the deposit from the buyer
Estimating all costs		
	Advising on mortgage offer	Advising on mortgage offer and organizing money transfers
	Filing the transfer of title document	

as specialist subject, however, people who become licensed conveyancers are also allowed to practise, even though they are not fully qualified solicitors. Every conveyancer has to carry out a variety of procedures, which are outlined in the table opposite.

Client care

Over and above the standard service they should provide, good legal firms/ individuals will send out a brochure, leaflets or a 'client care letter' explaining the legal process, the time frame and details of the costs involved. They will also clearly set out all the charges relating to the legal process and offer a complaints procedure if you are not happy with their service at any time. In this computer age, it is helpful to ensure that a conveyancer can email you the latest information on your purchase/sale.

Good communication

Although transferring a title doesn't take long, what does take time is the amount of communication required between you, the conveyancer, estate agent, local authorities and the mortgage company. Questions, forms and follow-up have to be actioned once searches or contracts have been received. Multiply this by an average individual caseload of 100+ cases and this explains why some people complain of receiving a bad service when using a legal firm/individual. Often, a case does not become a priority until near exchange or completion date. Also, a large caseload is usually the reason why an individual cannot come to the phone or return your calls, which is why email can be the best form of communication.

good to know

Points to look for in a conveyancer
▶ Because of all the organization and liaising entailed, you will need a firm or individual that is able to multi-task, handling lots of different cases at different stages while prioritizing those that are close to exchange and completion.
▶ Good legal firms/individuals should have a system whereby they can update you either by phone, email or letter. It is really important to ask how they manage their communication with you and other companies they have to liaise with.
▶ Ideally, you need to quiz the legal firm on how many cases an individual is expected to handle at any one time. Any firm that says more than 100 cases is likely to have difficulty giving enough time to your case, particularly if any problems occur.

Exchange and completion

The main frustration sellers/buyers experience is that to complete contracts you need first to exchange them. So when you set a date for completion (moving in), this can only be done on exchange. Sometimes a simultaneous exchange and completion can take place, but this is rare. Most completion dates are achieved, as there are penalty clauses if they are not. Unfortunately, there are no penalties for missing an exchange date. As a result, few conveyancers exchange on the date agreed as all too often one of the legal firms/individuals in the chain will find 'extra work' to do, questions that should have been asked or deposits that are not ready, and the process is thereby delayed. When choosing a legal firm or individual for conveyancing, check how they would ensure contracts are exchanged at least two weeks before your ideal completion date.

Different types of conveyancer

As with estate agency chains and mortgage companies, some of the largest conveyancing or legal practices are owned by companies who tend to offer 'shed' conveyancing where you may not be given a specific person to deal with your case but a call centre number. Equally, many such companies may outsource your business to a chosen panel of solicitors or licensed conveyancers. Other legal firms may operate at a local level and have a specialist department for conveyancing or only do conveyancing work.

Better customer service

Over the last five years, new types of conveyancing company have emerged that place greater emphasis on providing good customer service. Most of these companies operate via the internet, backed up by call centres and online 'case management' systems. These companies have pioneered 'fixed fee' and 'no sale, no fee' conveyancing. They set out all the costs of the process so that you have a complete understanding of what is involved.

Costing

Legal fees for buying and selling a property vary dramatically. Those for buying are higher than for selling as there is more for the legal representative to do and more services to purchase. You also pay more the higher the price of the property and for a leasehold property – which involves more work for the conveyancer.

The table below sets out average costs for the legal services entailed in buying and selling a property. Fees can vary considerably from company to company, however. Using a licensed conveyancer can be cheaper than using a solicitor, and remember that more companies are using 'fixed fee' and 'no sale, no fee' conveyancing, which enables you to work out your budget for the legal costs of buying and selling a home.

Legal fees for buying/selling a property

Sale for the sum of £150,000 in England/Wales	Fee (inc. VAT)
Sale fee	£560
Indemnity policy contribution	£ 30
Land Registry office copy entries	£ 8
Telegraphic transfer fee	£ 35
TOTAL	£633

Purchase for the sum of £250,000 in England/Wales	
Purchase fee	£ 500
Searches, etc. (approximate cost)	£ 150
Bank transfer fee	£ 30
Land Registry fees	£ 220
Indemnity policy contribution	£ 35
Stamp duty	£2500
TOTAL	£3435

Choosing a surveyor

The importance of having a survey done on a property cannot be emphasized enough. It is rare that a survey will conclude that a property requires no work on it and, because of what may be entailed, you will be given the chance to renegotiate the offer price, and thus cover the cost of having the survey done.

What a surveyor does

Most surveyors carry out a similar job as they are all professionally qualified and they must adhere to certain codes of conduct. Unlike many of the other services, the company or the individual can be sued if you have a valid claim against a surveyor who has missed vital issues, such as subsidence or the presence of damp, which should have been picked up at the time of the survey.

Types of survey

We have already mentioned (see box on page 34) the two types of survey that can be carried out, namely the homebuyer's survey and the building survey. The building survey is more detailed and sometimes more specialized than the homebuyer's report.

A homebuyer's report: the surveyor values the property, taking into account its location and condition and the research they have carried out.

A building survey: the surveyor doesn't necessarily give a valuation, but does list all of the work that needs to be done and gives an estimate of how much this will cost. See the checklist opposite for an outline of the minimum amount of work that a surveyor will undertake to make. Once you have the survey, it is then up to you whether you wish to use this information to reduce the agreed offer price.

Minimum requirements for a survey

The surveyor needs to do the following:

- ▶ Organize a date and time to visit the property.
- ▶ Either pick up the keys from the agent or go directly to the vendor.
- ▶ Visit the property to check:
  - levels of damp on floors and walls
  - internal and external wall structure
  - drainage system
  - age of the plumbing and wiring
  - signs of subsidence
  - state of the décor
  - quality of bathroom(s) and kitchen
  - condition of doors, windows, and extensions or add-ons
  - roof structure internally and externally from ground level
  - road in which the property is located, plus the surrounding area.
- ▶ Gain comparable details of similar, recently sold properties and their value.
- ▶ Produce a report that:
  - summarizes their physical checks on the property
  - indicates whether further surveys or information are required to confirm their findings
  - indicates what renovation work is required/recommended on the property now and in the future
  - advises on whether the property is meets latest building regulations
  - comments on the surrounding area and any issues that might affect the price, such as bus routes, busy roads.
- ▶ Advise on the cost of rebuilding the property in case of damage.
- ▶ Answer any queries that you may have.

Caveats in a survey

One of the frustrations with surveyors is that they are rarely able to give you a full idea of the property's condition. This is because they cannot carry out checks on the plumbing or wiring, or behind carpets or boarding. As a result, there will inevitably appear to be a lot of 'caveats' in their report, plus recommendations for further surveys that need time to organize and may increase the cost. A survey is still worth having, however, as the purchase of a property is such a big investment. In addition, it is important to follow up on anything that the surveyor recommends such as surveys on timber and damp. Most of these are free and give a more detailed view of any underlying problem, as well as providing a more accurate picture of what the cost will be to fix the problem. All of this can, if necessary, be negotiated from the final offer price.

Looking for the right surveyor

When looking for a good surveyor or practice, the key points to note are the level of communication and time they will take to survey the property. A good surveyor will:

▶ Contact you prior to viewing the property.

▶ Discuss whether there is anything that you are concerned about or want them to investigate.

▶ Discuss their report and any queries you may have.

▶ Check whether there are any special access requirements at the property being surveyed.

▶ Agree to let you go around the property while they survey it, sharing their findings as they go.

▶ Not include lots of 'standard' paragraphs in their report.

Insurance policies: Some companies even offer an insurance policy within the price of the survey, which protects you if the property then exhibits a problem that the surveyor did not pick up. You may have to pay slightly more for such a survey, but it provides instant protection and peace of mind and shows customer consideration.

Time taken for a survey: Another way of comparing companies is to look at the time they estimate they will spend on a survey. A homebuyer's report should take a minimum of two hours. A really good surveyor, however, will take up to four hours, bringing ladders to check any accessible roofs (especially flat roofs) or guttering, rather than rely on a visual inspection only. A building survey can take anything from half to a full day, depending on the size, age and condition of a property. A good surveyor will try to inspect timber or walls in detail, rather than just doing 'spot checks' around the property.

Some surveying practices require their surveyors to carry out a targeted number of surveys per day, especially if a mortgage valuation report is required, as well as the survey for you. This is clearly something to watch out for, given that it may therefore restrict the amount of time they spend surveying a property for you.

Cost of a survey on a residential property

The cost of a survey can vary from a few hundred pounds to over £1,000. To reduce the fee, you can instruct your mortgage lender to carry out the survey at the same time as their

good to know

Home information packs

Due to changes in the Housing Act of 2004, having a survey of a property before it goes on the market for sale is likely to become a legal requirement. The Act sets out that every home that is marketed for sale will require a 'home condition report' to be carried out and made available to potential buyers before they make an offer on a property. These changes – which represent the most significant in the industry for the past 20 years, completely changing the way we buy and sell property in England and Wales – are likely to be tested during 2006, but are not expected to become compulsory prior to 2007.

The key issue that has yet to be resolved is who will pay for this report to be done. It is likely that England and Wales will follow a similar system to that of Scotland where a new type of surveying process has been adopted. Buyers typically obtain a survey of a property prior to making an offer so there is no time lag and buyers and sellers are more prepared at offer and acceptance stage than in England and Wales.

Both the Surveyors and Valuers Association (SAVA) and RICS have set up a training scheme to create 'home inspectors' to provide details for the pending 'home information packs'. The student will have to gain an academic qualification from a college or university before being admitted to training for the home inspector diploma.

mortgage valuation on the property. Many offer a reduced cost if you agree to use the same surveyor for both. This is not always the case, however, and it is important to find out the cost and talk to the surveyor that you will be instructing before agreeing with this, as well as checking how long they will take to conduct the survey. Some of these companies require their surveyors to deal with a higher number of calls per day than a local practice would do, which reduces the amount of time they can spend at any one property.

The cost of a homebuyer's or building survey is influenced primarily by the type of property (whether a flat or house), its size (usually indicated by the number of bedrooms) and the price you have

Example of survey costs: flats

Type of report	Under £250,000		Between £250,000 and £500,000		Over £500,000	
	Up to 2 bedrooms	Over 2 bedrooms	Up to 2 bedrooms	Over 2 bedrooms	Up to 2 bedrooms	Over 2 bedrooms
Homebuyer's survey	£300	£400	£400	£450	£500	£600
Building survey	£550	£700	£600	£800	£850	£1,000

Example of survey costs: houses

Type of report	Under £250,000		Between £250,000 and £500,000		Over £500,000	
	Up to 2 bedrooms	Over 2 bedrooms	Up to 2 bedrooms	Over 2 bedrooms	Up to 2 bedrooms	Over 2 bedrooms
Homebuyer's survey	£400	£500	£550	£600	£650	£800
Building survey	£600	£900	£700	£1,000	£900	£1,300

Surveyor checklist
- Will they send you information about the work they can/cannot do?
- Is their work insured if they miss something?
- How much time will they spend surveying a property?
- How long do they spend on a
  - homebuyer's survey?
  - building survey?
- How much does each cost?
- What area do they cover/specialize in?
- Do they specialize in checking:
  - old properties?
  - environmental factors, such as a tendency to flood?
- What qualifications do they have and how long have they been surveying?
- Do they adhere to a code of conduct?
- What is their complaints procedure?
- Will they give an independent valuation of the property and/or estimated costs to put things right?
- How long will it take to produce the report once the survey has been done?

offered. Other factors would include the age of the property and the number of buildings to be surveyed on the plot. All surveys are subject to VAT, so do not forget to add on 17.5% to the quoted costs. The tables opposite give an indication of how much each survey would cost.

Other costs: If you are required to organize extra surveys, such as a structural survey or one to examine timber, damp or infestation, again the costs can vary from nothing for timber and damp to £100 per hour for other reports. It is best to budget £500 or more for additional surveys.

Choosing an insurance company

The insurance company provides a suitable policy that protects you if something happens to the physical structure and fixtures/fittings of your home, or its contents, providing funding for any repairs or to replace items that have been damaged, lost or stolen.

Buildings and contents insurance

When buying and selling a property, buildings insurance is compulsory if you need a mortgage, and contents insurance is advisable but not a requirement. For the buyer, buildings insurance has to be in place at the time of exchange of contracts and you will need to give your conveyancer the policy number and details. In the past, the provider of buildings and contents insurance has tended to be the mortgage lender. When a lender gives you a quote for your mortgage, they normally send out a quote for buildings insurance too, as the mortgage valuation of the property includes the cost of rebuilding your home should anything happen to it. But in the last ten years, insurance companies have created policies for buildings and contents insurance that have made the market much more competitive and driven down the costs. Hence you don't have to accept the quote from your mortgage lender.

Regulation

The insurance market is similar to the mortgage market, and there are over 9,000 companies to choose from. Many mortgage companies also offer insurance services. As with mortgage companies, there are a mixture of different bodies – insurance companies, insurance brokers and independent

Buildings and contents insurance checklist

When buying buildings insurance, you need to check the following:

- What is the excess?
- How the insurance company will fund any rebuilding of the property, i.e. replace it or rebuild in its current construction/form.
- Whether they provide accommodation while you are waiting for essential repairs to be done.
- What level of accommodation you can expect.
- Whether they offer a 24-hour help line.
- Whether they make interim payments or pay for the accommodation themselves.
- How quickly they will investigate and settle your claim.

When buying contents insurance, you need to check the following:

- What is the excess?
- Whether they replace the items as 'old for new'.
- Whether the quote includes accidental damage.
- Whether your valuables are insured in transit, such as when you go on holiday.
- Whether items above a certain value require additional cover.

financial advisers – all of whom can sell insurance. Also, just as with mortgage companies (see page 52), insurance companies now come under the regulation of the FSA, albeit it a little later – since January 2005.

Under these new regulations, any company or individual selling insurance will have to adhere to the FSA's guidelines in the processes they follow and written information they give, and quotes must set out charges clearly and in a way that is easy to compare with those of other companies.

What an insurance company does

Whether you have found a property or not, you can still choose which insurance company you want to instruct. You would need to estimate the value of the property that you are looking to buy, the area in which you'd like to buy a property (including a nearby postcode), and what the likely building cost and value of the contents will be. On average, the building cost of a property is 75% of the value of a home, although this can vary.

Most companies follow the same procedures but some are better at explaining what is and is not included in a policy. This is an important issue when choosing which company to use, as it can account for why costs vary.

did you know?

Obtaining a quote
The best way to obtain a reasonably accurate quote for an insurance premium is to use one of the online calculators (see page 81) or ask a financial adviser, insurance broker or intermediary to give you some guidance.

Risk factors

The insurance company will assess any environmental factors such as subsidence, a tendency to flood, the proximity of landfill sites, or the presence of naturally arising gases – all of which may increase the risk of damage to the property. All these factors will be taken into account when they give you a quote. Some companies, however, only take on low-risk properties and may not quote for old properties; ones near rivers, and hence more subject to flooding, or even a second property or holiday home that is left unoccupied for much of the time. So if you are buying a specialist property, you should search early for the right insurance company to find the best quote for you.

Choosing the right insurance company

While you are obtaining quotes from insurance companies, it may be difficult to work out which is the best company to go with because you will only discover how good their customer service is when you have to make a claim. The key points to watch out for are:

▶ A special telephone line for customers wanting to make a claim.
▶ A 24-hour help line.
▶ Claim forms (ideally ones that can be downloaded from the internet).
▶ A target number of days to:
  – send out your claim form
  – settle your claim.
▶ Contact details of the individual who would be dealing with your claim.
▶ Clear information about what is not covered by the policy.
▶ Help to gain quotes for the work that needs to be carried out, or have their own companies do the work.
▶ Guarantees on any repair work carried out.
▶ 'No claims' discounts.
▶ Whether they vary their insurance premiums based on excess fees.
▶ An independent arbitration process for any disputes.
▶ Whether you pay by lump sum or monthly instalments.

Insurance costs

The main insurance costs that you will incur are for buildings and contents premiums. The cost of insuring your property and contents varies for many reasons, such as the postcode of where you live or the number of claims you have made in the past. As a result, it is very difficult to give an estimate for an 'average' or 'standard' premium.

When obtaining quotes for insurance, it is important to gain quotes from a wide range of companies. All insurance companies have different claims experience, so those who have been heavily hit by flooding claims may charge more than others who have not been so hard hit.

Another reason for shopping around for quotes is that companies may base the premium for buildings insurance on the amount quoted by the surveyor, on a fixed cost or on what they estimate it would cost to rebuild the property. Contents insurance is exactly the same and the cover can be based on your estimate of contents value, or a set or an unlimited amount. This can be in your favour if there is a very high build cost or costly contents, as 'unlimited' cover can be more cost effective than an exact amount.

must know

Insurance company checklist
- Have they been approved to sell insurance by the FSA?
- What qualifications do they have?
- Do they adhere to a code of conduct?
- What happens if you want to complain?
- How will they value your property/items?
- Do they offer both contents and buildings insurance?
- Do they clearly lay out the monthly/annual insurance costs; what they do/don't cover and what the claims procedure is?
- How long does it take for a claim to go through?
- Will you be put up in a hotel/other accommodation of your choice should something happen to your home?
- Do they find you contractors to do the work?
- Do they require three quotes from you for such work to be carried out?
- Do they settle directly with the company?
- Do they reimburse you instead?
- Do they offer a contents policy that is 'old for new' or current value only?
- What commission do they gain from you placing your insurance policy with them?

Choosing a removal company

A removal company will transport your belongings from the property you are selling to your new home. On the surface, it may seem like something you could easily do yourself – pack up your belongings in a few boxes, hire a van or small lorry, load everything and drive off. The reality can be very different.

Energy saving

An average removal requires 100–150 boxes, all carefully packed to prevent breakage, and includes heavy items and pieces of furniture that may need dismantling or careful handling around corners or down the stairs. As a rule, if you have more than two bedrooms and/or any large items of furniture that may be difficult to move, it is worth using a removal company rather than attempting to do it yourself.

The main point to consider is not how much money you could save by doing it yourself, but how much time it will take you. You also need to work out where you will get the packing materials from, the cost of van/lorry hire and how much help you can get from friends and relatives.

What a removal company does

The standard service provided by a removal company is outlined opposite. Removal companies that 'go that extra mile' tend to train their staff; offer a higher level of customer service; include a level of insurance for your goods in case there are any accidents or you are unexpectedly delayed and adhere to their own, or an associations, code of practice (see below). In addition, they will have an arbitration policy should things go wrong, dismantle (and put together) furniture/items if required and be accredited with the European Standard for household moving (BS EN 12522).

Codes of practice

Many of the companies that offer these extra levels of service take their role in the moving process very seriously and belong to the British

Association of Removers (BAR) or other European or global organizations such as Federation of European Moving Associations (FEDEMAC) or the International Federation of International Furniture Removers (FIDI). These associations require their members to give a certain standard of service and stick to a code of practice that is independently monitored.

Training and qualifications

There is no regulation or requirement for anyone to run a removals company. Most removal companies, however, also transport house contents abroad, undertake commercial moves, import and export goods and manage fleets of lorries and vans. As a result, they do need a great deal of specialist knowledge and skill to manage all these different aspects. Within the industry, an arm of BAR is the Movers Institute, which runs training and accreditation for individuals.

When you are choosing a removal company, check if they are members of any of these associations. Also establish whether your goods are insured against damage and whether their staff have received suitable specialist training.

Removal costs

As with insurance, the cost of removal can be hugely variable. Moving the belongings of someone with a minimalist lifestyle will obviously not cost as much as moving those of a compulsive hoarder! The cost can be broken down into four basic subdivisions – loading and unloading, insuring, packing and storing – so be sure to outline your requirements when getting an estimate.

must know

Basic tasks of a removal company
- Sending someone to visit your property.
- Filling in a form detailing all your belongings and estimating:
  - volume of items needing to be removed
  - number of boxes required
  - size of the removals team needed
  - size of lorry and number required
  - time it will take to pack and load your items
  - journey time to the new property
  - value of your items (if insuring).
- Considering any issues with loading/unloading, such as no off-street parking and ease of access into the property.
- Sending out a written quotation.
- Securing transport and staff for the day.
- Unloading/unpacking the items at the new property.
- Storing the items at an agreed location.

Moving home – doing it all yourself

As long as you have the time, make sure you check that you are working within the law and covering every aspect of the move, it is possible to do it all yourself, but it would be wise for a legal firm to check that you have done your conveyancing correctly as this has huge implications if you get anything wrong.

Legal guidelines for selling your property

Many people manage to sell a property themselves through advertising on the internet or in the newspapers, or by putting their own 'for sale' board outside the house. In addition, it is helpful to produce 'sales particulars' for potential buyers, along with photographs, room measurements and your contact details. However, you must stick within the legal guidelines when advertising your property for sale.

There are two areas where you need to ensure that you stay on the right side of the law. The first regards the 'for sale' sign that you put up outside your home. You are only allowed to use one board or two joined together. If you are using one board, you can have a different advert on each side. The size of the board is also restricted to 0.5 square metres in area, or a total of 0.6 square metres for two joined boards.

Estate agents that advertise properties have to ensure that the sales particulars produced are accurate or they will be committing an offence under the Property Misdescriptions Act. This does

good to know

Sales particulars
It is helpful to produce these for buyers so that they don't 'forget' your property once they have left. You will need to include:
▶ Indoor and outdoor photographs.
▶ A short description of the location and accommodation, including:
  – number and type of rooms
  – room dimensions (using metric measurements)
  – number of windows per room
  – telephone, electric and TV aerial points.
▶ Anything included in the sale, such as carpets/curtains.
▶ Garden, garage, outbuildings.
▶ Your contact details.

not apply to individuals selling a property, but you should ensure that you make accurate statements or this could lead to problems before or after the sale.

Advertising your property

Since the advent of the internet, selling a property yourself has become much easier. You can order a 'for sale' board, advertise on specific 'private sale' websites, and some people even create their own website for their property. However, it is unlikely that you will reach enough potential buyers just by promoting your property on the internet and by a board outside your house. In addition, you should consider advertising in:

▶ Your local property paper.
▶ *Loot/Daltons Weekly.*
▶ The property sections of national papers.

You could even expand your advertising to your place of work or another venue, such as your local supermarket, post office, sports or other club, that you think might help reach potential buyers. Bearing in mind that 80% of people tend to buy within a three- to five-mile radius, it is worth trying to cover this area in your advertising.

As long as you are careful and make the estate agent aware of your own efforts to sell your property, it is possible both to use an agent (under 'sole agency') and advertise privately. If you can prove to the estate agent that you have found a buyer through your own advertising campaigns, then this is perfectly legal and hence going down both routes – advertising yourself and using an agent – can help maximize your opportunity to gain a buyer.

Showing viewers around yourself

It is not really enough just to show someone around your property saying, 'Here is the kitchen, here is the dining room ...' It is much better to try and think of ten points you love about the property to say while taking a potential buyer around your home. Explain why you like a room, what its features are – such as sunny in the morning, the views

or its privacy. You can use the time you spend
walking around the property highlighting what you
are leaving behind or point out the average costs of
running the property on the way around, such as
average heating bills, water rates, council tax.

Receiving an offer

If you receive an offer, make sure you ask what the
buyer's circumstances are. Have they sold yet, are
they first-time buyers, have they applied for a
mortgage? If you accept their offer, you need to ask
for their conveyancer's details and draw up a letter
to send to the buyer and both their and your legal
representative, confirming the acceptance of the
offer, the offer value and any terms and conditions
pertaining to the sale of the property.

You will then need to keep an eye on the
progression of the sale – checking with the buyer
that they have their mortgage offer and discussing
any issues that might arise from the survey.

DIY conveyancing

Doing your own conveyancing is possible, but you
need to make sure you carefully follow each step of
the process. As previously stated, it is a good idea to
get a solicitor to check that you haven't missed
anything out.

DIY financing

This is much easier to organize these days, as there
is lots of help from the internet and magazines such
as *What Mortgage?* or *Your Mortgage.* Using these
sources, you are able to compare different types of
mortgage or insurance premium, which are the

monthly costs, what they include or exclude, excess payments and any penalties.

You will have to be sure of what type of mortgage or insurance package you want and have some idea of what 'features' you require, such as an account in which you pay no penalties for moving to another insurance company, or 'accidental' cover for your house contents.

DIY removal

If you are doing this yourself, the earlier you start the better. You can easily purchase boxes and packaging material from the internet or storage companies. Work out how many boxes you will need and the approximate volume of goods you will be moving so that you can decide how big a vehicle you need. You will need to measure the largest item you have, its width and height and depth, so that you know it will fit in the van.

Type of removal van: Removal vans come in all shapes and sizes. A basic driving licence permits you to drive a vehicle up to 7.5 tonnes (or eight seats). This is equivalent to a Luton van, which has extra packing space over the driver's cabin. In addition, you will also need large blankets or sheets to protect your belongings.

Timing: Ideally, your vehicle should be packed and ready to go by lunchtime. It isn't a good idea to rely on a completion time that allows you to load the items from your current property and unload them into your new one, then come back for more. Your property sale is likely to go through prior to your purchase. So make sure you have a big enough vehicle to cater for all of your contents in one go.

Other services

If you want to maximize the value of your property, move quickly or just don't want to spend your valuable time buying and selling a home, there are various sources of further help that you can secure to move home.

Auction houses

Traditionally, auctioning your property was something you would resort to only if the property was in a great state of disrepair or if you were a professional developer and needed to buy land or a large or unusual property, or wanted to get rid of a property quickly. In addition, repossessed properties are usually sold through auction.

Selling and buying a property via an auction house does have distinct advantages over using an estate agent, however (see box below), and is becoming increasingly popular.

What auction houses do

The role of the auction house is no different from that of an estate agent in that they act on behalf of the vendor and aim to secure the best price from the most appropriate buyer. The main difference is that the process takes place on a set date and once a sale is agreed during the auction, the buyer has to give their deposit there and then and is legally committed to completing in a set period of time – usually 28 days – or you get to keep their deposit.

---

must know

Key advantages of using an auction house
- Exchange and completion within four weeks.
- Securing a bargain or gaining a price higher than on the 'open market'.
- Dealing with buyers who have their finances ready.
- Selling post-survey – not before.
- Dealing with people ready to sell, who are unlikely to 'pull' their home off the market.
- Once a price is agreed, the buyer cannot renegotiate.

Basic tasks of an auction house
- Visiting your property.
- Recommending a 'minimum sale value' or a 'reserve price'.
- Producing sales particulars.
- Adding the property to their list of 'lots'.
- Taking potential buyers and a surveyor around the property.
- Securing the deposit (typically 10%) on the day of auction.
- Running an auction and taking bids.

Qualifications: Auctioneers typically have a degree and specialize in a certain subject – such as property, fine art or china. Their qualifications are more like those of a surveyor as they often take on this role prior to becoming an auctioneer as it helps them advise on achievable and reserve prices. So look out for 'FRICS' or 'MRICS' ('fellow' or 'member' of RICS) after their name for proof of qualification.

Auction costs: Selling your property at auction costs about the same as via an estate agent – approximately 2% of the final value achieved on the day. In addition, you have to pay for inclusion in the auctioneer's catalogue. There are other costs to bear in mind too, for, if you are selling, you have to have instructed a solicitor to draw up contracts for sale prior to the auction.

When buying, you also incur charges whether you purchase a property or not. Before the auction day, you may have to pay for a catalogue or list of properties to view. In addition, you will also have to instruct a surveyor to obtain a value for the property; instruct a conveyancer to gain information about planning, searches, etc.; put your finances in place so you can complete within 28 days; and agree with the auctioneer what method of payment they will accept for the 10% deposit.

Buying agents

If you really do not want or don't have the time to trawl around the estate agents for property details and then visit them one by one, you can ask someone else to do this for you. Buying agents are either self-employed 'one-man bands' or work for a 'home search' company. Typically, someone who acts as a buying agent will obtain most of their business from company relocations as the cost is funded by the company.

Qualifications: There are no qualifications for a buying agent, but if they work in relocation they may be members of the Association of Relocation Agents and therefore have a code of conduct that they have to adhere to. The best way to make sure you are choosing the right person to work with is through referral from friends, clients or companies they do relocation work for.

must know

Basic tasks of a buying agent
- Meeting with you to understand what it is you are looking for.
- Obtaining property details from estate agents.
- Viewing properties on your behalf.
- Recommending properties f or you to view.
- Advising on an offer price.
- Securing the property for you.

Pros and cons of using a buying agent: There are several advantages to using a buying agent, in that they generally know all the estate agents well and may gain information about suitable properties either before, or as soon as, they are on the market. As buying agents search for properties, usually within a specific area, they become knowledgeable about property prices within the area and can advise on the best offer price. The downside of using a buying agent is that they may only search for properties at a minimum value – say £500,000 – and they typically work on a commission basis of approximately 1.5% of the value of the property. You are also likely to have to pay several hundred pounds to retain their services and may incur charges even if they cannot find the property you are looking for.

Home staging

Thanks to Channel Five's 'House Doctor' Ann Maurice, the American import of 'home staging' is now an established industry in the UK. You can choose to do this yourself, but many local interior designers are expanding into this market and companies such as Home Stagers (see page 81) are setting up a nationwide version.

There are clear benefits of changing your home to make it more saleable. In a slow market, it can make the difference between your property staying on the market or selling relatively quickly. In a good market, it can help improve the desirability and therefore the price of the property.

Qualifications: Interior designers would typically have a qualification, such as a diploma or degree, and local clients whose work they can show you and can recommend them. They would also have a 'portfolio' of work with photos and case studies for you to see and check that you are happy with the type of style they are likely to create for you.

Cost of using a home stager: Costs range from £50 per hour to a day rate of around £500. Although this may at first seem high, remember that the person helping you should be able to secure all the items that they

recommend and have trusted local tradesmen who
can carry out the work, saving you enough time to
justify spending the money.

Storing your belongings

This is an increasingly popular service to choose
when buying and selling a home. When selling a
property, it is helpful to use a storage facility if you
have already 'grown out of' your home and are
moving to gain extra space. Otherwise the property
may look cluttered and give the impression of being
much smaller than it really is.

Advantages: The benefit of keeping your
belongings in storage is that most of the companies operate locally on
a nearby industrial estate. They provide 24-hour access and offer flexible
space and access to your goods. They usually have a range of container
sizes and give you – or you may have to purchase – your own padlock and
key. The company can advise you on how much space you will need, based
on the number of rooms or bedrooms you have in your property, and now
they also supply and sell packaging materials, such as bubble wrap and
boxes of every size. They usually have good access for large vehicles as
well as cars, and have trolleys that you can use to help save you time and
effort shifting your goods.

Cost of storage: This will be approximately £200 a month for a 15-
square-foot area, which should be big enough for the contents of an
average three-bedroom property. The minimum amount of space you can
hire for storage is usually 10 square feet. In addition to storage facilities,
removal companies also provide storage. Your removal company is likely
to have its own facilities and will quote for storage, or there are national
storage companies such as Big Yellow or Access Storage, as well as locally
based companies who may be able to offer more competitive rates.

The key points: Check the company has good security, it adheres to
fire and safety regulations, and you can gain access to your belongings at
a convenient time. Check, too, the notice period for removing your goods.

Choosing an estate agent

Check in the Yellow Pages or the property pages of your local paper, or contact:
National Association of Estate Agents (NAEA)
tel. 01926 496800
www.naea.co.uk

Ombudsman for Estate Agents
tel. 01722 333306
www.oea.co.uk

Royal Institute of Chartered Surveyors (RICS)
tel. 0870 333 1600
www.rics.org.uk

For Acts of Parliament affecting estate agents, contact the Office of Public Sector Information
tel. 01603 723011
www.opsi.gov.uk

Choosing a mortgage company

The Financial Services Authority (FSA) regulates the mortgage market:
www.fsa.gov.uk/consumer

To help find your way through the mortgage maze, try the Council of Mortage Lenders (CML):
tel. 020 7440 2255
www.cml.org.uk

To find an independent financial adviser contact IFA Promotion (IFAP):
tel. 0800 085 3250
www.unbiased.co.uk

A good source for the latest financial information is the Sunday papers or buy a specialist magazine such as *Your Mortgage* or *What Mortgage?*.

Choosing a legal firm for conveyancing

The Law Society gives advice on choosing a solicitor for conveyancing:
tel. 0870 606 6575
www.lawsociety.org.uk/home.law

The Council for Licensed Conveyancers (CLC)
tel. 01245 349599
www.theclc.gov.uk

Companies such as Easier2move have an online calculator to assess conveyancing costs. In addition, they will organize a solicitor to act on your behalf for a set fee:
tel. 0700 432 7437
www.easier2move.co.uk

The Land Registry has more information about the future of conveyancing in the UK:
tel. 0870 908 8066
www.landregistry.gov.uk/e-conveyancing/

Choosing a surveyor

The Royal Institute of Chartered Surveyors (RICS) has a section for the public on their website:
tel. 0870 333 1600
www.rics.org.uk

The Independent Surveyors Association (ISA) offers advice:
tel. 0800 970 8521
www.surveyorsweb.co.uk

For more information about the Housing Act of 2004, contact the Office of Public Sector Information (OPSI) (see above)

Property Industry Research Ltd tracks and gives information about the home condition report:
tel. 01202 890988
www.hicb.co.uk

Choosing an insurance company

The Association of British Insurers (ABI) have an 'information zone' on their website:
tel. 020 7600 3333
www.abi.org.uk

You can find insurance companies or brokers by looking in the Yellow Pages or your local newspaper. Contact the FSA to make sure a company is fully qualified and accredite:
tel. 0845 606 1234
www.fsa.gov.uk/firmcheckservice/index.html

To compare or gain insurance quotes, visit:
www.insuresupermarket.com
www.1stquote.co.uk

Choosing a removal company

For help finding a removal company, contact the British Association of Removers:
tel. 020 8861 3331
www.removers.org.uk

To compare quotes on removals, log onto:
www.bishopsmove.co.uk
www.houseremovals.com

Federation of European Moving Associations (FEDEMAC)
www.fedemac.com

International Federation of International Furniture Removers (FIDI)
www.fidi.com

Moving home – doing it all yourself

Which? provides useful information and a 'Home Mover's Guide':
www.which.net/moveit/takecontrol/diy

You can purchase key conveyancing packs for around £30 online from:
www.questbrook.co.uk

Websites that will help you sell your property include:
www.houseweb.co.uk
www.propertybroker.co.uk

Other services

Fulfords (auction house)
www.fulfords.co.uk

Auction locations across the country:
www.property-auctions.net

Association of Relocation Agents (buying agent)
tel. 0870 737475
www.relocationagents.com

Stacks (buying agent)
tel. 01594 832880
www.stacks.co.uk/

Home Stagers
tel. 0800 542 8952
www.homestagers.co.uk

Access Storage (storage companies)
tel. 0800 731 8404
www.accessstorage.co.uk

Big Yellow
www.bigyellow.com

Dealing with problems

The Citizens Advice Bureau has a guide to problems that may arise when dealing with any of the services involved in the buying and selling of property, and can give independent advice:
www.adviceguide.org.uk

3 Planning and preparing to move

Moving home is ranked as one of the top three most stressful types of experience in our lives next to divorce and losing a loved one. With so many people involved and different stages, it can be difficult to control the process. We need someone who is looking to buy at the time we want to sell our property and at mutually agreeable prices. Then we have to choose from thousands of companies to help us through the process. Aaargh! But worry no more: this chapter explains how to take control. Careful planning makes a huge difference, helping to banish the stress and ensuring that every stage proceeds as smoothly as possible.

Step-by-step guide

Familiarize yourself with each step laid out here and understand what has to be done by everyone involved. You can then take charge of the purchase and sale; spot potential problems before they arise; have time to solve problems if they happen; and create back-up plans to save stress and hassle.

1 Do you really want to move?

One in every three offers accepted to buy or sell a property falls through. The main reason for this is that many people start the process by looking for a property, but then decide that they either cannot afford what they want, or that their own property is still their best option. Use the local property paper or internet to help make sure the type of property you are looking for is out there at a price you can afford before you start the process (see pages 18–19 and 22).

2 What location and specification of property are you looking for?

Many people confuse what they want with what they can afford. And many change their minds about the specification they originally gave the estate agent, wasting time and money in the process. Make sure you research carefully whether you really want an old or a brand new property, one with a large garden or a renovation project. Then check that you can afford this type of property in the area you are thinking of moving to before you start making visits. Do 'drive-bys' of properties you are interested in and research the additional running costs of the property you want before you brief an estate agent.

good to know

Precision counts
Be reasonably precise in the specification you give an agent. For example, don't say 'two bedrooms' if you need two double (i.e. good-sized) bedrooms. At the same time, don't place too many limitations on the spec. If you need two double bedrooms, but would like three, ask for a minimum of two double bedrooms – otherwise you may limit the properties that you receive in your price range.

3 What is the value of your property?

If you have to sell your own property to buy a new one, it is essential to research how much it is worth. Check how much similar properties are in the local paper/on the internet. Then check whether they are selling – and how long it takes. Talk to local estate agents and check property price surveys for how much properties have actually sold for (see pages 18–19 and 22).

4 Check your valuation with local estate agents

Once you are fairly sure how much your property is worth, or if you cannot find a comparable property, ask a minimum of three agents for a valuation. If they come back with prices that vary by more than 5%, then ask two more agents for their view and take an average of the prices they recommend as a guide for how much your property is worth on the market (see page 31).

5 What is the minimum/maximum price you would accept?

Once you know the value of your own property, check with several finance companies to see how much they would be willing to lend you. Ideally get a mortgage agreement from one of them in principle (see page 53). Also check if there are any restrictions on the percentage of the property price they will lend on.

6 Preparing to sell

It is tempting to visit properties before you have done any research or even put your own on the market. This can cause problems as you might see a property you like but then miss out as someone else is in better position to purchase than you. Make sure you prepare your own property for sale before you start looking for another one.

7 Putting your property up for sale

Once you have given the go-ahead to your agent to sell your property, it can take a few weeks for it to be advertised in the local paper or for details to be mailed to potential buyers. After this, it can take a month or more to receive an offer on your property. Make sure you give yourself the best chance of selling before you fall in love with another property – put your home up for sale before you look at any others.

8 Choosing a conveyancer
Once someone has made an offer on your property or you have made an offer yourself, it can take four weeks or more for the contracts to be drawn up by the legal representative of both parties. You must also take time to choose a conveyancer before you make an offer (see pages 56–7), so you are not rushed. If you are selling and certain you are going to move, you can even have your contracts of sale ready by the time you receive an offer, saving weeks for all concerned. If you are buying, you can choose and instruct a legal firm/individual prior to finding a property, so that you will be ready to give their details to the agent if your offer is accepted.

9 Registering for property lists
Subscribe to as many different sources as possible – internet sites (see page 38), estate agents and the local property paper – to give yourself every possible chance of seeing properties that are up for sale.

10 Finding a property
Set aside four to eight hours a week to search, book appointments, view properties and surrounding areas. After viewing each property, let your agent know as soon as possible what you liked/disliked, so that they can help pinpoint properties that will suit you best. If necessary, alter your specification, not forgetting to change any saved searches on the internet on sites such as Rightmove (see page 38).

11 Making/Accepting an offer
It is possible to accept an offer even if as a seller you have not found a home. It puts you in a good position if you do then find a property to buy. Just make sure that you definitely want to move and that you know there is a property out there you want and can afford. Otherwise everyone, including you, will be wasting time and money.

12 Informing your finance company
If your offer on a property is accepted, inform the finance company immediately of the address of the property and your conveyancer's details.

13 Organizing a survey

Surveyors can take up to two weeks to book an appointment to view your property – so inform them as soon you have received the acceptance letter of the offer from the estate agent. Brief them about anything you are concerned about and want investigating. Check how they should gain access – either by ringing the estate agent or the vendor. (See pages 60–5.)

14 Agreeing dates for exchange and completion

Many people think this is entirely down to the conveyancer, then find after a few wasted weeks that it isn't. Talk through with your conveyancer at the start how long they think it will take, as well as gaining a view from the vendor either directly or via the estate agent. Then suggest a date for exchange and completion and make sure the estate agent or conveyancer puts this in writing to all parties. If everyone agrees, you can now all plan for those dates, or agree mutually acceptable dates.

15 Dealing with the paperwork

Once offers are accepted, there are property forms and mortgage applications to fill in, title deeds and Land Registry documents to check, identity and credit checks on buyers and sellers to be carried out. At this time, the crucial contracts of sale are created, ready for exchange and completion. Deal with all of the paperwork promptly as this is one of the main areas that holds up the process.

16 Finding a removal company

Brief at least three removal companies (see pages 70–1), obtain and compare costs and choose which one you want to move your belongings. Inform them of your likely completion date and, if you sign any contract with the removal company, make sure it is done 'subject to exchanging' contracts on your sale/purchase.

17 Exchanging contracts

This is a crucial point in the moving process as it confirms the price of the sale/purchase and

must know

Deposit monies
You must have your deposit monies cleared with your conveyancer in order to be able to exchange contracts, so make sure you have the money ready in time.

confirms that everything is going ahead. The legal representatives of both parties confirm the exchange of contracts, but you need to have checked, signed and returned (ideally by hand or special delivery) the final documents.

18 Preparing for moving day

Make a list of things you need to do:
- ▶ before the big day
- ▶ on the day
- ▶ after you move.

19 Organizing your move

Once you have exchanged, you can confirm the completion date with your removal company. If selling, inform your utility providers of your completion date – in writing. Ideally book a meter reading for the completion day to ensure an independent reading for your final bill. If buying, make sure the vendor does this, or do it as soon as you have moved into the property.

20 Informing about change of address

Some companies take weeks to alter change of address details. To help save you time, organize your post to be redirected for a minimum of three months. You can inform some companies two weeks beforehand, some only on the day and some can wait until after the move. You can even be fined for not notifying the DVLA in sufficient time. (See page 101.)

21 Organizing children or pets

Moving day is stressful with lots to do and coordinate. If you can, send children or pets to a friend for the day as it can be very difficult looking after them at the same time as packing or being on hand to advise the removal team.

22 Having a clear-out

If you have lots of items you do not want to take with you, take them to the tip, or even hire a skip. Defrost your freezer and run down food supplies before you move, throwing away anything that is out of date. It will save a lot of time and effort on the day of the move.

23 Getting ready for packing up

Set up an easy system for the removal team. Brief them on the layout of the new property, make sure fragile or precious items are easily identified and make clear in which room certain items should be placed in the new property.

24 Clearing up afterwards

Make sure you leave out cleaning equipment and arrange for one person to stay behind to clean the property and another to leave with, or before, the removal team set off. Leave out refreshments such as drinks, a kettle, cups, milk, sugar and snacks.

25 Completion

Your conveyancer – who handles all of the finances such as the monies for the deposit, the mortgage and paying your estate agent – deals with this. Once contracts are completed, the conveyancer should ring you and let you know that you can enter your new home or must exit your old one.

26 Sorting out your new property

- ▶ Clearly mark each room as per your plan – e.g. Bedroom Two, Dining Room, Playroom.
- ▶ Check and write down any meter readings.
- ▶ Check you know where the stopcock is, how to work the heating system, that you have all the keys you need for the windows, doors and padlocks.
- ▶ Clean the property if required before you move in.

27 Tying up loose ends

- ▶ Inform any remaining friends/neighbours/companies (such as magazine subscriptions, catalogues) of your change of address.
- ▶ Make sure your conveyancer registers you as the new owner of the property with the Land Registry.
- ▶ Check whether you want to stay with your current utility companies or switch to a cheaper service in the area.
- ▶ Register yourself on the electoral register and for your new council tax. Also, organize with your previous local council any refund of tax you may be due.

Time plan

Estimating how long it will take to buy and sell a home is a bit like calculating the length of a piece of string. This is because every move is different and most moves take place as part of a chain. Most sales rely on a purchase and are expected to happen on the same day, however many people are planning to move.

Being part of a chain

The chain outlined in the box below will stop if the person selling property five moves into someone else's home, leaves the country, passes away, owns the property as an investment or if there are other circumstances that mean their sale is not reliant on moving into a property on a set date. The longer the chain, the more difficult it is to exchange contracts. If you cannot exchange contracts, you cannot complete.

As a result, the whole chain can only exchange and therefore complete when every single buyer/seller, conveyancer and mortgage lender has done everything they need to do to confirm the purchase/sale. If one person or conveyancer is not ready, no one can move. If they have forgotten to ask certain questions on the day of exchange or the mortgage company has not arranged for the money to be drawn down, exchange cannot take place.

It is possible to monitor or shorten the chain to make your move an easier one if you use a time plan to manage the moving process.

---

good to know

A typical chain
- ▶ Property one: first-time or cash buyer purchasing.
- ▶ Property two: being sold to person selling to the first-time buyer.
- ▶ Property three: being sold to person selling property two.
- ▶ Property four: being sold to person selling property three.
- ▶ Property five: being sold to person selling property four.
- ▶ Person owning property five not buying a new property.

How to plan your move

Although you cannot control the time frame of the entire chain, you can, before you even start selling or looking for a property, have a time plan that you would like to work to. With this in mind, you can then:

▶ Monitor the sale and purchase so that you know what might affect the time frame and for how long.

or

▶ Shorten the chain to make the process more likely to fit within your time frame.

Speed of buying/selling

One of the key influences on how long it takes to buy and sell a property is what is happening in your locality, especially with regard to the type of property you are looking for. At the beginning of the millennium, for instance, the buying and selling process was very quick as property prices were rising so fast.

Taking the chain and the speed of the market into consideration, if you are buying, you should set aside a period of 3–6 months for the whole process from planning to moving in. If you are buying and selling, you should set aside a period of 6–12 months. It can happen much faster than this, within 6–8 weeks. But this would depend on you finding the property you want at a price you are happy to pay, and the same applies to someone you are selling to. This time frame can increase/decrease depending on the speed of the market.

The reason for setting aside this much time is to make sure that you make due allowance for any problems and to ensure that the move is less stressful, with less likelihood of having to make decisions under pressure.

There are average times that it takes for the key stages of the moving process and these are highlighted in the table overleaf. Please note that this timetable does not include any of the pre-planning stage, which will take an additional 4–12 weeks, depending on how straightforward your move proves to be.

Timing of the different stages of buying/selling	
Making an offer on a property	4–8 weeks
Selling a property	4–12 weeks
Obtaining a survey	2 weeks
Obtaining a mortgage offer	2–3 weeks
Legal searches	1–2 weeks
Legal contracts drawn up and signed	3–6 weeks
Exchanging contracts	3 weeks
Completing contracts	1–3 weeks
Minimum time overall	20 weeks
Maximum time overall	39 weeks

Ways of reducing the time frame

If you, your finance company, your buyer/seller and respective legal representatives are efficient, the whole process can be done in 6–8 weeks. If the property is sold on the agreement that the purchase will go through within a specified time frame, it gives the conveyancer and finance company a time frame to work with from the start, rather than you being put to the back of the 'queue'. Another way of controlling the time frame is to 'break the chain'. This can be done by either you, your buyer or the person you are buying from agreeing to move into rental or temporary accommodation. This ensures a smaller number of parties working together for a mutually convenient exchange and completion date.

Monitoring the process

If you are keen to stick to a certain timescale, you can refer to the key stages in the table above to help reduce the time frame and check whether everyone – up and down the chain – is keeping to the schedule. Although as a buyer you cannot speak directly to everyone else's legal representative, you can liaise with each of the estate agents who then contact either the solicitor or the individual buyers and sellers. Some estate agents will do this for you, but if they do not or you would prefer to do it yourself, it helps keep a check on which property purchase/sale is at which stage.

For example, after four weeks of your offer being accepted, check that all the conveyancers have produced or are close to producing the property forms and the contracts for buying and selling. If this has all been done, check whether any specific questions have been raised and, if so, whether they had been answered. Then double check which exchange date everyone is working to – just in case someone has a different date in mind. If you find any issues at any stage, either contact your estate agent or conveyancer to advise them of the problem and gain an answer as to how and when the issue can be rectified.

---

good to know

Other ways of reducing the time frame

The vendor
- ▶ Draws up sale contracts as soon as they put a property on the market.
- ▶ Conveyancer draws down the deeds of the property from the mortgage lender.
- ▶ Property 'fixture and fitting' and 'information' forms filled in as soon as an offer is agreed.
- ▶ All forms are sent to the buyer's conveyancer within two weeks of the offer, then passed on in the third week to the buyer.
- ▶ All paperwork is either delivered/picked up on the day it is ready or sent by special delivery.
- ▶ Answers all the buyer's legal questions by return.
- ▶ Agrees to a maximum of two weeks from exchange to completion.

The buyer
- ▶ Obtains a mortgage agreement in principle.
- ▶ Checks that the mortgage company's ability to lend does not rely on certain conditions, such as:
  - – age of property
  - – condition of property
  - – type of property (e.g. a house converted into a flat)
  - – their circumstances (e.g. self-employed, reliance on bonuses or commission).
- ▶ Instructs a surveyor to survey the property within a week of the offer being made.
- ▶ Searches are applied for as soon as the offer is accepted, or they use an agency or online access facility.
- ▶ Asks all their questions within a week of the forms and contracts being sent to all parties.
- ▶ All paperwork is either delivered/picked up on the day it is ready or sent by special delivery.

Preparing your home

If you are selling a property, unless it is in perfect order and completely clean and tidy, then it is best to prepare your property – and yourself – for your pending move. Everyone has different requirements, but normally people move for more space or to downsize. Few move to the same type of property, so there is usually work to be done.

Jobs that need finishing

It is important to understand how buyers view a home. They usually make their decision on whether to buy or not the moment they step foot in through the front door. When we live in a house we get used to things that we mean to 'get around' to doing. When selling a home it is essential that you do them

must know

Buyer 'put-offs' checklist

The following are essentials that need to be sorted as they often frighten buyers into thinking that there is more work than actually required. They can also be picked up by surveyors and influence the valuation on your home, or suggest that more surveys are required.

- Poor or bare wiring.
- Lights without lampshades.
- Cracked kitchen or bathroom units.
- The smell of damp or unsightly damp patches.
- Hard-water/limescale marks.
- Cracks in walls, ceilings or floors.
- Leaking drainage or pipes.
- Dripping taps/showers.
- Draughty windows or doors.
- Dead plants.
- Unpainted areas such as new plaster.
- Polystyrene tiles on ceilings.
- Exposed asbestos.
- Leaking roofs or water 'sitting' on flat roofs.

or it may affect the price a buyer will offer. If necessary, ask a friend or neighbour to come and point out things for you – better to hear it from them than put off a potential buyer!

If you have any of the items listed in the box opposite, then your property is likely to take more time to sell and consequently a savvy buyer may try to offer much less than it would cost to fix any of these items.

If it is not needed – chuck it out!

When you are looking to move, you can help make your home look its best just by throwing away things that you do not need. This increases the amount of space the house has to offer. It is hard if you have children who have lots of toys to play with, or you like to collect things or hate throwing anything away. If you have not used it, worn it, played with it in the last 12 months, you must consider whether you really need it. If not, put it away in a box or into storage during the viewing period. If you realize after a certain time that you do not need it, you can then throw it away.

The best place to start is your garden shed, garage, loft space and cupboards. No doubt you will have put things away that you have forgotten existed. The more these spaces are cleared, the more the buyer will feel there is room for their own belongings.

One of the main areas to look at is your kitchen. Unless you are very efficient at using up whatever you buy from your local shop or supermarket, then you are bound to have items in your cupboard that are out of date and cannot be eaten. Take the opportunity to clear the freezer out at this stage too. The real benefit of throwing items away is that, when you come to move, the quote from the removal company should be cheaper than if you had kept everything.

good to know

Key places to clean

▶ Remove any grease, grime or limescale from the kitchen area.

▶ Clean or buy new sink bowls or bins if they currently look overused.

▶ Make sure there is no mould in the bathroom/kitchen or other areas.

▶ Dust and vacuum the property thoroughly.

▶ Rid the property of any strong smells.

▶ Clean glass, including windows and shower enclosures.

▶ Clean taps and around sink waste.

▶ Throw away any dead plants.

Cleaning the property from top to bottom

It is an obvious statement, but buyers really notice whether a place is clean or not. We all have different measures of cleanliness, but if you do not make the effort to clean your property, a buyer will worry about what else you have 'forgotten' or not done, and lose interest.

Ensuring the garden/outside space looks its best

Unless you have a stunning property or a particularly large garden, you will need to make sure it is presentable front and back. No one is expecting a 'show home' garden. What people do expect, however, is that:

▶ Lawns are mowed.

▶ Dead plants or weeds are removed.

▶ All rubbish and garden waste is removed unless you have a compost heap.

▶ Any outbuildings such as shed or brick building are clean and tidy.

▶ Water features/ponds are clean.

Ideally, most people like somewhere for children to play safely and an area where they can put a barbeque and sit to eat.

Maximizing the internal space

When maximizing the space buyers see, it is very important to make sure that it corresponds exactly to the sales particulars. How rooms and space are described to buyers in the particulars is extremely important. If the details describe your property as having three bedrooms, for instance, viewers will expect to see three rooms with beds in them. This might be because they have two children or are hoping to let a room to a lodger or have a spare room for guests. If they then see two good-sized rooms and a box room used as a study or storage space with no bed in it, most will automatically assume a bed will not fit.

Buyers would also expect to see furniture that is 'to scale' with the room. For example, a king-sized bed in a 3m by 3m (10ft by 10ft) room, leaving little room for a wardrobe or anything else for that matter, would put buyers off. If necessary, take any over-sized furniture out while you are selling to show the rooms to their best advantage.

Whatever your space, never leave anything out on floors, tops of wardrobes or elsewhere as it gives the impression that the property does not have enough space for 'everyday' items.

Setting a standard for your property

When selling a property, buyers will purchase it either because it is decorated or laid out exactly as they want and to their taste, or because they feel they can buy at a price that allows them to create the environment they want. What is very difficult to sell – and price – is a property that is 'half done'. A property that has a brand new kitchen but requires a new bathroom can limit its appeal and will reduce its desirability.

It is also important to show that the property you own would cater for any look that a buyer might like to give it. For example, if someone were buying an old property, they would typically want to see 'character' features, such as coving, fireplaces and old doors. If someone is buying a brand new property, they are likely to want to see the latest trends. Alternatively, if someone wants to renovate a property, they may prefer little work to have been done to the house before they purchase.

If you are not sure what to do to maximize the appeal and value of your property, then ask your estate agent or call in a local interior designer or someone who specializes in preparing a property for sale (see pages 78–9).

Preparing the paperwork

One thing we all underestimate is the amount of paperwork that piles up day after day when in the process of buying and selling a property. The paperwork has recently increased, unfortunately, as has your responsibility to complete it – you could even be fined for not completing it accurately.

Be organized

Organizing the paperwork for your pending move and keeping it filed in one place (see box below) and means that you can find everything you need when you are asked. This can dramatically speed up the process of moving home and reduce the frustration of not being able to get things done because you have not got the right information or papers to hand.

good to know

Filing your paperwork
The best way to organize your paperwork is an A4 lever-arch file – you will fill it by the time you have finished your move! Set the file up to include sections as follows:
- List of contacts.
- Property sale.
- Property search.
- Finance information:
  – mortgage
  – insurance.
- Conveyancing.
- Survey.
- Removal.
- Utilities.
- Change of address.
- Miscellaneous.

Homebuyer's information packs
Check when these are due to be introduced before you look to sell your home. Ask your local estate agent and conveyancer or log onto the website www.odpm.gov.uk. Due to revisions in the application of the Proceeds of Crime Act of 2002, the Money Laundering Regulation of 2003 and Data Protection Act of 1998, you now have to:
- Prove your identity.
- Provide information on where you gained your funds to buy/afford a property.
- Sign up to agreements to allow you to receive property details.

When the homebuyer's information packs come in, vendors will also need to prepare their contracts for sale, along with property forms and a specific survey on their property – all that before the property can even come onto the market!

List of contacts

It is really useful to have the contact names, telephone numbers, email, fax and address details of all the different companies you are working with. Keep a copy in your 'master file' but also give one to anyone else involved in the move. Keep a copy at work too, as you never know when you are going to find a property you want to offer on or when you might receive an offer. No work can start until you have given all the contact details of your conveyancer to your estate agent.

Property sale

Keep the information that the estate agent has given you. This should include:

► Estate agent contact details.
► Letter from the estate agent confirming the marketing price and their costs.
► Copy of the signed terms and conditions of the estate agent's services.
► Copy of any offers, whether accepted or not, that the estate agent must put in writing to you.
► Your sales particulars, including spare copies in case a potential buyer turns up without them.

Property search

Keep all the details of properties that you like filed. Ideally file them with 'favourites' first. Record on a sheet of paper what you liked and did not like about a property you visited. This also means you will have the details of estate agents that are selling the type of property you are interested in, so you can call them weekly to see if they have any more properties on their books.

Finance information

Make sure that you keep this information secure, keeping a copy of your:

► Current mortgage company details.
► Mortgage account number and/or 'roll number'.
► Mortgage valuation report.
► Completed application form for the new mortgage.
► Confirmation of your mortgage offer.
► Current insurance company details.
► Policy details for buildings and contents insurance for your new property.

must know

Before exchange of contracts
If buying, ask your conveyancer to make sure that they request all of the information you want or anything you are concerned about and need clarification on prior to exchange of contracts.

In addition, check whether your insurance policy covers your belongings during the move.

Legal information

Your conveyancer cannot do any work for you unless you have provided them with proof of identity, and typically a cheque for approximately £250 to cover searches, which they have to purchase. They require either a valid passport or driving licence with a photograph, as well as a recent utility bill with your name and current address.

If you cannot deliver these to your conveyancer by hand, then you can have copies of them certified by a qualified accountant, local solicitor, doctor or bank manager, and send them by post.

Your conveyancer will also require the following contact details/information:

▶ Your buyer's/seller's conveyancer.
▶ Your mortgage company.
▶ Your mortgage roll/account number.
▶ Buildings insurance policy details for the new property.
▶ Copy of your survey.

Paperwork that you will need to have to hand from your conveyancer will be:

▶ Contract of sale.
▶ Contract of purchase.
▶ Copies of title deeds of the property you are purchasing.
▶ Copies of the 'property information' and 'fixtures and fitting' forms for both the sale and purchase.

Survey

▶ Letter of instruction confirming the type of survey you have requested and the price.
▶ Copy of the terms and conditions you need to sign and return with payment.
▶ Two copies of the survey (one for your conveyancer).

Utilities

It is really helpful for potential buyers to know the likely running costs of your property. If selling, you will also need to provide the utility details for the moving day as well. The key papers to have are:

▶ Council tax band and cost.
▶ Buildings insurance costs.
▶ Water, gas, electricity – including details if you are on Economy 7 plus the details of which companies you have used.
▶ Oil – including the company you have used and the frequency of deliveries.

Removals

▶ Details of the quotes you have received.
▶ Contact details of the removal company you have chosen.
▶ Copy of their terms and conditions.
▶ Confirmation of the removal date, time they are going to turn up and price.
▶ Any insurance that you may need to claim after the move.

Change of address

It is amazing how many people and organizations you need to inform about your change of address and very easy to lose track of the relevant paperwork when in the throes of moving. The best way to ensure you have all the details of the people/organizations you need to inform is to draw up a checklist as soon as you intend to move, including account or reference details where necessary. You will have to contact some companies to request their own forms, as some do not accept notification of change of address via a standard letter.

Some companies give away free information, folders or standard forms/letters to help you get through all the paperwork, so ask your estate agent or conveyancer if they provide these.

Preparing finances

Organizing your mortgage prior to house hunting or making an offer is one of the most important stages of the home-moving process. In fact, one of the major reasons why one in three sales fall through after offer stage is that finances are not in order and so mortgages cannot be secured.

Step by step

The first step in gaining a mortgage is to sort out what your income and outgoings are. The table left gives an idea of the sort of information that will help a mortgage lender decide how much to offer you. Don't forget to include anything that you have bought on hire purchase or any other loans you may have. Lenders will check for these and you are required to provide this information. And don't forget to add in any income that you may receive such as bonuses or other monies you can prove are regular income to the mortgage lender.

Income and outgoings
Income
Salary 1
Salary 2
Allowances/benefits
Pension1
Pension 2
Other income
Expenditure
Housing costs
Council tax
Utility bills
Insurance
Car costs
Food costs
Saving plans
Subscriptions
Hire purchase
Holidays
Going out
Clothing
Other
Income minus expenditure

Proof of income

Once you have a true idea of your income/expenditure, then you will need to provide proof to the mortgage lender of your income. Many lenders will request this information from your employer directly, but you can short-circuit this by asking your employer to prepare the letter confirming your earnings prior to offering on a property.

Self-employed: If you are self-employed then finding a mortgage lender willing to give you a loan isn't so straightforward. In order to agree to lend you money, most lenders require three years of accounts or Inland Revenue self-assessment tax returns, particularly if you are a first-time buyer. If you haven't been in business that long, you can still secure a mortgage, but you may be expected to offer a higher than normal deposit on the house or pay a higher rate of interest on the loan.

Self-certification mortgage: Another option, if you have a variable income that is difficult to prove, is a 'self-certification' mortgage. This allows you to give your income and expenditure without proof of earnings as long as you sign a declaration to say it is accurate. You will be credit-checked to ensure you have met previous commitments and the lender may verify with your accountant or bookkeeper that your statements are correct.

The self-certification mortgage may appear to be a licence to ask for whatever mortgage you like or give an exaggerated impression of your earnings. It is important to remember, however, that if you make false or misleading statements, you risk legal action. Also, if interest rates rise quickly and you cannot pay for the mortgage, you risk losing your home.

Poor credit history: People with a poor credit history – for whatever reason – will also be checked by the mortgage lender and this can influence their decision whether to loan you money or not. Your credit history is built up over time from when you take out a credit card, loan, make payment to utility companies or to pay off a previous mortgage. Any default in payment is recorded on your credit rating. Companies then license access to this information to check your credit rating prior to lending you money. If you have any county court judgements or have missed mortgage payments or undergone bankruptcy, these will subsequently stay on your file for six years and severely limit the number of lenders that will be willing to give you a mortgage.

It might be that there is a good explanation for why you have a bad credit history. As long as you can prove to the lender that you are doing your best to rectify the situation, then you can still have a mortgage. However, the likelihood is that you will be charged a much higher interest rate – several percent higher than anyone with a good credit history would pay. This can make a big difference to the size of the mortgage a lender will be willing to offer, so it is crucial to check your borrowing power before you start looking for properties.

Mortgages – seeing the wood for the trees

We are bombarded daily with information and advertising about mortgages. The internet now provides us with sites that can compare thousands of mortgage products, information about interest rates, deposits required, application costs, penalties, discounted rates and much more.

Before you even start to look for a mortgage, the first thing to decide is how you want to pay back your mortgage over time. This is in fact an easy choice as there are only two options – repayment and interest-only.

Trying to set up a mortgage yourself with the help of the internet or specialist books and magazines is much easier nowadays. But as independent financial advisers (IFAs) and mortgage brokers have access to a greater range of mortgages, it is worth shopping around yourself and then asking an IFA or broker to do another check – as long as you do not have to pay upfront for the work. This way you get the best of both worlds and can check your findings against those of the specialists.

Repayment mortgage: With this type of mortgage, the money you pay back each month pays partly for the interest on the loan the mortgage lender is charging as well as paying back part of the money that you have borrowed. The monthly and annual payments are based on the money owed, interest charged and the time you take to pay the mortgage back. The result is that if you take a mortgage out for 25 years, at the end of that period you will have paid off your mortgage. Generally speaking, if interest rates move up or down, so will your monthly repayment.

Interest-only mortgage: This mortgage only requires you to pay the lender the interest on the money that they have lent you. At the end of the loan period – say 20 years – you have to repay the mortgage lender the amount that you have borrowed. There are two ways of doing this. You can sell the property and, providing the value is the same or more, pay the lender back all the money you borrowed and pocket any excess. If your property is worth less than you borrowed, then you will have to make up the difference. Alternatively, you can set up a savings plan at the start of the mortgage loan (such as an endowment policy, ISA or PEP), and repay the lender from that plan at the end of the loan period.

It is your decision which of these options you choose. On the whole, repayment mortgages require higher payments per month than interest-only mortgages. With an interest-only mortgage, the lender normally requires that you set up savings plans to ensure you can pay back the mortgage and retain your property at the end of it. This can mean that your total monthly payments are exactly the same as for a repayment mortage.

With interest-only mortgages, you do run the risk of the investment not saving as much as required to pay back the lender. This happened recently with some endowment policies. Some haven't performed as well as anticipated, leaving several thousand people with not enough savings to pay back the lender.

Mortgage offers
Once you have decided on which type of mortgage to go for, you can then look at the different packages on offer from the mortgage

lenders. Everyone's personal finances are different, so it is important to take independent financial advice before you choose any mortgage deal.

There are various different 'packages' that mortgage lenders offer. These can broadly be divided into the following:

Interest rate deals: The interest rate driver for these deals is the 'base rate' – the amount that the Bank of England sets each month that determines the percentage at which banks can borrow money themselves. The base rate is usually below the rate that lenders lend money – and that is how they make their profit from you. If the base rate goes up, your mortgage interest rate usually follows. If it goes down, your mortgage interest rate may or may not go down by the same amount, as mortgage lenders sometimes use this to increase their profits. The types of rates are outlined in the box below.

Off-set account: This is a relatively new type of account that enables you to lump together the majority of your finances. For example, you may have a current account, a savings account and a cash ISA. The idea of an off-set account is that all of these are placed in one account. You can thus draw money down or pay off your mortgage depending on your circumstances. This can result in lower

---

must know

Mortgage interest rates

Variable rates mean that as the base rate goes up so will your mortgage interest rate and therefore your monthly repayments and vice versa.

Fixed rates mean that your interest rate and monthly payments remain the same, usually for a set period of time, whether the base rate goes up or down.

Discounted rates usually mean that your mortgage interest rate is an agreed percentage below the lender's variable rate. For example, if the lender's variable rate is 6% and you have a 2% discounted rate, you will pay 4%.

Capped rates mean exactly that – if your capped rate is 6%, for example, then the interest rate will never exceed that rate for the time specified by the lender. If the rate falls below 6%, you pay the lower rate.

Tracker rates ensure that your repayments will stay plus or minus a certain amount, e.g. 1% of the base rate, going up or down according to its movement.

monthly mortgage repayments as the amount owed goes up and down according to expenditure and savings. During hard times, mortgage 'holidays' can be taken; during good times, the mortgage can be 'overpaid' without incurring any penalties.

Cash back: This type of mortgage promises to pay you a sum of money once you have taken out the loan. For example, if you take out a £150,000 mortgage and the offer is '1% cash back' you will receive £1,500. It is important to check the rate of interest you will be paying or the amount you have to pay for the mortgage application to assess how much of a benefit this will be to you.

Mortgages with multiple applicants

Nowadays, with people tending to buy property later in life, living together when not married or even having to buy a property with friends to get onto the first rung of the property ladder, more 'multiple' applications are being made to mortgage lenders.

There are two ways in which you can purchase a property jointly:

Joint tenancy: This means that two people purchase a property in their own names, but if one dies, then the other part of the property goes to the surviving person. This usually applies in the case of a husband and wife.

Tenants in common: This means that when more than one person buys a property and one of those people dies, then the portion of the property they own passes to their estate. This may mean that on death the property is required to be sold, unless other legal stipulations are made.

It is important to discuss which is the best way of applying for a joint mortgage with your financial adviser and your legal representative to make sure you make the right choice and are aware of what might go wrong.

Conveyancing and tax

Sorting out everything you need on the legal front is important to ensure the purchase and sale of your property proceeds as smoothly as possible. Paperwork is generated from contracts and forms, and starts even before you sell your home or make an offer on another property.

Make time to check everything

Dealing with the paperwork can be a lengthy business, so you need to put aside time to go through everything you receive from your conveyancer. There are cases, for example, where vendors have taken away items that purchasers believed were included in the sale. Unless you carefully check the information you provide and receive, important details can be missed.

Registered title deeds

The deeds of a property show its boundaries within a street/building plan. They also list previous owners and what they paid for the property. From the deeds you can see if the boundaries conform exactly to the area of land/building you believe you are buying. For example, the current owner may have access to park his or her car on land that is owned by someone else. This may be withdrawn if an agreement is not in place for it to continue or may reduce the amount you are willing to pay for the property.

Fixtures and fittings form

This form is filled in by the vendor and clearly lays out what is and isn't included in the sale. This can be one of the biggest areas of dispute when buying and selling a property. It is both the vendor's and buyer's responsibility to ensure that they agree exactly what is being left/taken as it can affect the final price of the property. For example, you may love the curtain rails, blinds and curtains and think they are included in the sale price. The vendor, meanwhile, may be of the opinion that you should pay extra for them or that they are taking them with them. They may even change their mind halfway through the proceedings. Once filled in and checked by both parties, this form makes it clear from the time of exchange what is and isn't being left.

The form states too that you are responsible for removing any rubbish and all possessions not highlighted in the form. If you do not, then the buyer may decide not to complete until you have done so and you may incur penalty charges. Equally, if the vendor takes items that you had previously agreed would be left, you may claim compensation for them.

Vendor's property information form

This is a very informative, but very long and complicated form to fill in. As with the fixtures and fittings form, it is part of the contract of sale/purchase, so make sure you take time to complete it. In addition, it is a good idea to hang on to the form as you may need it next time you come to sell or move. See right for what is laid out in the document.

Property searches

This is an enquiry to various authorities to find if there is anything that is likely to affect your property in the future, such as a new road or flight path, which may make the area much noisier, or the risk of flooding. The search also checks for planning applications, building control certificates or if the property is situated within a conservation area or there are any tree preservation orders. In short, it ascertains what might prevent you from using or developing the property as you would wish, such as building an extension. Finally, it checks for radon and any hazardous substances that may have been placed below ground that could affect your ability to make changes to the property. It may mean that the surveyor has to ensure that correct procedures have been carried out, such as suitable membranes laid to protect the property from leaking gases.

Buyer's questions

These are additional questions that the buyer's conveyancer asks that are not covered by the property forms or searches. They are a relatively new addition and might include such things as: Where is the stopcock? Whose are the utility companies? Can you confirm the water rates? To ensure you know where everything is, ask your estate agent to make an appointment for you to meet with the vendor to go through such points. If there is any point to do with the purchase that you are still not sure about, make sure you ask your conveyancer quickly to avoid delay in exchanging contracts.

Contract of sale/purchase

This brings together all of the above forms and summarizes the agreement to 'convey' the property from one person to another and requires your signature(s). It includes all names, addresses and any issues that have been highlighted through the legal searches. Also included is the price at which the property is being bought and the rate of interest to be applied should either side not complete or delay the process after exchange.

Completion of registration, office copy entries and filed plan

These are forms that you should receive from your conveyancer after the contract of sale. The plans lay out the boundaries of the property you own, the title of the land and its history of ownership or any grants for rights of way. They are particularly important to check through if the property you have bought has had its boundaries changed or if it is a newly registered property.

Stamp duty

A specific property tax paid is when you purchase a property. This used to be called stamp duty and is now referred to as 'stamp duty land tax'. It is your responsibility to fill in, sign and send off this form, although your conveyancer should prompt you and can help you fill in the information (see below).

The form includes information on who is selling and buying the property and their legal representatives, and the level of stamp duty being paid. Different rates apply, depending on how much you are paying for the property you are buying, and these are laid out in the table right.

In December 2003 a new system for paying stamp duty was introduced that requires you to fill in a form entitled STLD 1. Your conveyancer would have handled the payment of stamp duty on your behalf previously, but now they either complete the form for you (at a cost of around £50), which you then have to check through and sign, or you fill it in, sign it and make a direct payment. This form has to be sent to a central address at the Inland Revenue, and you will be fined if it is not paid within 30 days of completing on the property you are purchasing.

Sale of a second property

You can only sell a property free of taxation in the UK if it is classed as your 'main residence'. Any other property will be subject to capital gains tax when you sell it.

The amount that you have to pay tax on will be the difference between the price you paid for the property and the price you sold it at. Everyone has a capital gains tax allowance that can be deducted if this has not been used for shares or other earnings. Other factors that determine how much tax you pay are the amount of income tax you currently pay, how long you have had the property for and any costs that may be deducted, such as those entailed in selling the property.

Taxing a second property is complicated and depends on your circumstances, so seek advice from a property tax expert to ensure that you understand the ramifications of buying and selling a second property.

watch out!

Tax rules
The tax rules regarding property in the UK have changed and can alter annually, so check with your conveyancer or the Inland Revenue before you move if there is anything else you need to budget for. For example, some legal firms are now charging an additional amount to fill in the STLD 1 form and you need to make sure you allow for this.

Preparing for offers

Only two out of three purchases go through after offer stage. Offers are not finalized until exchange and everyone finds this stage stressful. If you are buying, you want to offer the lowest amount you think will secure you the property. If selling, you want to advertise your property at the highest price you think a buyer will pay.

Decisions, decisions

The reality is that you should offer what you are happy to pay for the property and adjust that offer prior to exchange if your survey has resulted in more work than you thought was required. If you are selling, you can accept an offer and keep your property on the market if you feel someone else might pay more for it, thereby keeping your options open.

The bottom line is that the first offer given and accepted is not necessarily the final price. This can change right up to the day of exchange. It is dependent on the mortgage offer, the survey and anything else that might be found during the legal process that could affect the property price. Once you take this on board, then the initial offer and acceptance can be dealt with on a 'subject to' basis, leaving both parties time to change their mind.

Accepting an offer

Before you start even looking for a property, you should have an idea of what price you are willing to accept for your property. That price should not be a single figure but based on 'minimum and maximum' amounts. As we have already seen, different prices can be achieved for a similar house on a month-by-month or week-by-week basis depending on how many properties are up for sale and how many buyers looking.

Which offer to accept

As a rule, if you can afford to move and secure the property you want based on the offer that you have received, it is better to accept than reject it, in case you regret it later. This is particularly the case if you receive an offer that is close to, on or above the asking price.

However, if you do receive an offer and think that you would like more money, or are dependent on the additional money to afford the next property you want, then it is worth asking your agent if they can get the buyer to increase their offer. A familiar tactic is as follows:

▶ Asking price: £150,000
▶ Initial offer price: £140,000
▶ Split the difference: £10,000
▶ Ask for: £145,000

If the offer is below the offer price, rather than renegotiating the price straight away it can be worth asking a few questions instead. Is the offer price low because the buyer:

▶ Thinks the property is overpriced?
▶ Thinks work is required that you are happy to do prior to the sale?
▶ Has seen another property for less money?
▶ Cannot afford to offer a higher price?

These are helpful questions to ask as they can help determine if the buyer is just 'trying it on' or if they have good reason to offer less than the asking price. On this basis, the buyer may state that the property needs repainting and they estimate this would cost £5,000. You may obtain quotes that put this figure at £3,000. You could even offer to do the work if they then offer the full asking price.

This is the same if the mortgage lender or surveyor comes back with a list of work required. You have the option of rectifying issues raised to give peace of mind to the purchaser or lender so their reason for lowering the offer price is negated.

> **did you know?**
>
> **Buying and selling in Scotland**
> When buying and selling in Scotland, the bid price can be up to 40% more than the guide price and you need to have a surveyor value the property prior to giving your offer to the estate or property agent.

Multiple offers

If you receive several offers at the same time and the potential buyers appear willing to increase their offers, then you can use a 'sealed bid' system. This is similar to the Scottish system where you give a 'bid price' and offers are often in excess of the 'guide price' or the one that is advertised. Sealed bids or bid prices are required by a set time and date. You obviously need to take into careful account your financial position when you place a bid.

Do not make an offer unless the bids are 'subject to survey' or you need to do a survey beforehand. This is really important as you may offer too much and the lender might not back you. Meanwhile, you are likely to have entered into a legally binding contract that you cannot then fulfil.

Making an offer

Unless you are an experienced negotiator, it is difficult to let your head rule your heart when making an offer on a property. You have probably spent weeks or months searching, visiting lots of different properties, even losing out to other buyers and finally you find the property that you want. It is very important to stand back and research the property's value as much as possible before you make your offer. You can then offer 'subject to mortgage valuation and survey'. This means that if the survey should throw up any problems, you can try and reduce the final offer price – as long as you negotiate before exchange.

The other benefit of researching the price you offer is that you can give the estate agent a good reason for lowering the price. This makes it easier for them to recommend your offer to the vendor and gives you the best chance of it being accepted.

---

good to know

Negotiation skills

▶ When making an offer, do not just use the price to gain acceptance. Point out the benefits of agreeing to sell it to you. It might be that you are a first-time buyer, have nothing to sell, or can move quickly. It might be that you are prepared to wait for the vendor to find somewhere so can be flexible on completion dates. Any advantages you have over other buyers can improve your chances of your offer being accepted.

▶ Many people worry about gazumping. This is when a buyer's offer is accepted, the sale proceeds and then the seller accepts another offer, usually close to exchange. It happens in approximately 2% of cases. This is why some buyers request that a property is taken off the market once an offer has been accepted.

Preparing for your move

The best time to start preparing for your move is as soon as you put your house up for sale, or if you are certain that you will be making an offer.

Doing your own packing

Packing your belongings always takes a lot longer than you think. If you are doing the packing yourself, then clear areas currently used for storage, such as the loft, garage, spare room or outbuildings.

If your search/sale is going well, start packing away everything you do not need on a day-to-day basis, especially items that can easily be stored and are not used regularly. This might include books, magazines, electrical items and out-of-season clothing.

If you have lots of ornaments, pack them away carefully and mark the boxes clearly with 'fragile'. Ideally add cardboard between each layer. Make sure you pack the sides and bottom of the box with soft protective items such as pillows, cushions, towels, paper or bubble wrap. And make sure all boxes – whatever they contain – are taped up, top and bottom, so that nothing falls out.

Pack everything that you can, leaving out only what you need for the next few weeks. Leave enough cutlery and crockery, towels for washing and basic items for washing and cleaning plus a few changes of clothing.

If you are packing yourself, then you need to have packed most of your items by the night before you move. You need to be ready to start packing the van/lorry you have hired early in the morning.

If you are in a short chain, or are one of the first few properties in the chain, you need to be ready to move all your items out by lunchtime on moving day.

Paying someone else to do the packing

If you would prefer to live your life without disruption until a day or two before you move, then it is worth getting removal companies to quote for packing your belongings for you. This has several benefits:

- ▶ You lead a normal life up until a few days before you move.
- ▶ You can concentrate on other things.
- ▶ The removal company is responsible should anything get broken in transit.

Packing costs can vary, but are usually a few hundred pounds. Considering this includes all your packaging material, trained packers (if you go with a reputable company) and your items are insured if they are broken, then this is one service that can be extremely good value for money.

Day of the move

On move day, make sure your file of paperwork relating to the move is easy to find – for example, by the telephone. It is best to arrange for children and pets to be with friends or family for the day so you can concentrate on briefing the removal team.

No one can tell you exactly what time monies will be transferred and the property ceases to be yours. As a guide, most people, if being moved by a removal company, are ready to go the night before or by midday on the day of the move. Pack up your last items – and make sure that you have an overnight bag ready, just in case you do not manage to move in and out in one day.

Make up some sandwiches for lunch as you'll be too busy to stop. Have snacks and drinks available if you are moving your own items – it's hard work and you will need to keep up your fluid levels.

Property transfer

There is an assumption that if a completion date is set, then all the monies will reach everyone's bank accounts on the day. That may happen, but it will not necessarily take place at a time that enables you to move all your belongings into your new home.

If you are involved in a chain, especially one with more than three properties, and you are not one of the first properties, make sure that you have a back-up plan in case all the monies do not change hands in time. Arrange for somewhere to stay the night, if necessary. Plan to either let the hire company know that you may not be able to bring the vehicle back or discuss with the removal team what needs to be done if there is a significant delay.

Only hand over your keys when conveyancer confirms that all monies have been transferred and that ownership has passed to the purchaser. Don't put your vendor in an awkward position by asking to enter their property unless you are confirmed as the new owner.

Step-by-step guide

There are lots of ways of working out minimum and maximum property values of your home or a home you are looking for. The main UK property websites are:
www.findaproperty.co.uk
www.fish4homes.co.uk
www.rightmove.co.uk

To check if a property is environmentally sound, key the postcode into the following websites. More detailed searches on a property can be done for approximately £30:
www.environment-agency.gov.uk.
www.homecheck.co.uk

For advice about noisy neighbours, visit:
www.nhf.org.uk

A government website gives helpful advice and information on buying and selling a property:
www.direct.gov.uk

To check a property's council tax band and cost, put in the postcode or address at:
www.voa.gov.uk

Preparing the paperwork

For free help in changing your address, go to the following website (associated with the Post Office):
www.iammoving.com

For a free, downloadable checklist, go to:
www.fish4homes.co.uk

To arrange for your mail to be redirected, get a form from your local post office or download it from their website.:
tel. 08457 740740
www.postoffice.co.uk/portal/po

Preparing finances

The Financial Services Authority (FSA) has created a budget calculator for you to use on- or offline. For more information, go to:
www.fsa.gov.uk/consumer

Check your credit rating with the following website set up by the Credit Reporting Agency:
www.checkmyfile.com

Experian
tel. 0800 656 9000
www.creditexpert.co.uk

Equifax
www.equifax.co.uk

Conveyancing and tax

For more information on the new land tax stamp duty form or latest stamp duty rates, contact HM Revenue & Customs (HMRC):
tel. 0845 010 9000
www.inlandrevenue.gov.uk

To understand property tax, visit the following website, which has mini guides to give you an idea of how tax is applied:
www.taxationweb.co.uk

Preparing for your move

Many companies now sell boxes to move home, especially storage companies. You can also order moving kits online from:
www.a1box.co.uk
www.removal-supply.co.uk

4 Structure and layout

For most people, buying a property represents the biggest financial commitment of their lifetime. Yet when choosing which property to purchase, this major decision is often made in a matter of minutes. Before you decide you really want a particular property and what price to pay for it, you should research how sound an investment it really is. Most property purchases and sales follow the standard procedures that have been outlined in earlier chapters. Particular properties, however, such as flats, new build, self-build or housing association properties, raise issues that need additional checks and regulatory procedures.

Understanding the structure of a property

Once you have found one or two properties you are considering making an offer on, there are three checks to make. One: consider the property's layout. Two: look at its physical structure and how well it has been maintained. Three: investigate the surrounding area and the wider environment (see pages 130–5).

Property layout and orientation to the sun

The layout of a property can make the difference between living in a space that suits you well or becoming frustrated with the restrictions that it may place on you if it is not satisfactory. When looking at the layout of a property, it is important to consider both the internal and external space.

People generally like to make the best of the sun and ideally want a 'light and airy' home. Always ask, or work out, which direction the property is facing as this will determine if sunlight will come streaming into the house from first thing in the morning, or whether you will need to have the lights on for most of the time.

External space

Garden: Many people who want to buy a house will expect a garden – however small – to go with it. A large family home with a small garden is unlikely to fulfil the family's needs. If there is only a small garden, but the house is a good size, it might be worth checking what additional outside space is available locally such as a nearby park, recreation centre or field.

Parking: With increased car ownership, it is important to check what parking is available, particularly if there is no driveway or garage. If you are buying a property near a town centre, school or railway station, there may be restrictions on parking on the road or you may have to compete daily for a parking space.

Think too of the implications throughout the year of not being able to park outside your own home. For example, a large family home with no parking may seem acceptable for a few weeks over the summer, but when it is cold and raining nonstop, that walk to the property with all the weekly shopping may become annoying.

Properties that are overlooked

Being overlooked either in the garden or within particular rooms in the house, such as the living room, is something else to consider. When you are looking around a property, check the degree to which you are overlooked by neighbours and passers-by. It is possible to use blinds and net curtains to reduce the problem, but this may restrict the light in a room. One solution may be to switch rooms around so that everyday rooms are at the back of a property, rather than at the front.

Another downside of an overlooked property is that it may be noisier (see also page 134). The nearer it is to a busy road or pavement, the more noise there is likely to be. Heavy lorries thundering past or lots of passers-by can be very intrusive.

Internal space checks

One of the main issues to consider is whether there is enough space to cook, play and relax downstairs for everyone and then enough good-sized bedrooms upstairs. This is referred to as the property's 'balance'. For example, a property may have had its layout changed to allow an elderly person to live downstairs. This could limit the price of the property and it may take longer to sell, unless the changes are easy to reverse, as it narrows the potential market.

Another check to make on a property is the ease of access from one room to another. For example, is the kitchen near the dining room so it isn't far to carry dishes to and from the table? Also, check if it is easy for everyone to get to the bathroom, or whether one person is going to be kept up by nightly visits from the rest of the family. Finally, look at the access to the garden and any outbuildings.

Once you are happy with the layout of a property, then you should make checks on its physical condition to ensure it is a sound purchase and no expensive repairs are required.

Structural check

A property may appear sound at first sight, but it is rare for a building to be in perfect physical condition – unless previous owners have been fastidious about its upkeep. Some problems can come to light in a matter of months, while others might take years to surface. It is therefore important to identify as many problems as possible before you buy as this can have an impact on the purchase price. Depending on the age and size of a property, most problems can be fixed quickly and easily. Other problems, however, such as damp or subsidence, can take months to sort out, requiring expensive specialist solutions.

Whenever you are buying, it is essential to arrange for your own, independent homebuyer's survey or buildings report (see page 34). Before you even make an offer, however, there are potential problems that you can look out for yourself that may determine whether you make an offer in the first place or may influence the figure you decide upon.

Damp: This is the most common problem surveyors find when checking properties. There are many reasons why a property may be damp, and several different types of damp problem to look out for (see box opposite). If you like a property and are considering making an offer, look for a damp course on the outside walls, close to the base of the external walls, and ask for any damp guarantee certificates that the owner may have.

Rising damp

This is where the property either does not have a damp course or the current damp course has failed. The problem can only be fixed by inserting a new one. At worst, this may mean the plaster needs to be taken off internally to a height of one metre in the affected rooms, followed by redecoration once the plaster has dried out.

Signs of rising damp are:
▶ Smell of damp.
▶ Plaster coming off the wall.
▶ Wallpaper or paint peeling/cracking.

Depending on the extent of rising damp, the costs of repairing it can range from a few hundred to several thousand pounds.

Penetrating damp

There are many causes of penetrating damp such as a leaking roof, guttering or plumbing problems. Other common causes include vegetation or paving too close to external walls, allowing water to enter the property above the damp course. The longer an owner takes to notice and fix these problems, the worse the damage to the property.

Signs of penetrating damp are similar to those for rising damp, but can happen anywhere in the property from floor to ceiling. As long as the cause of the penetrating damp can be found and fixed, however, the problem should be resolved.

Some properties do not have enough ventilation in the bathroom or kitchen or in areas where laundry is dried. This can cause condensation and a 'mildew' effect, mostly near windows or above the shower area in a bathroom. Installing adequate ventilation should resolve this particular problem.

Waterproofing a property: There are many ways that water can enter a property and it is important to make sure that everywhere is watertight. When putting a property up for sale, or when looking to buy a property, check the following:

▶ Guttering: look for cracks in joints.
▶ Roof: look for problems such as missing tiles and holes in the roof and make sure that joints are solid.
▶ Chimneys: check to see if you can see any damp around the bottom bricks or any cracks where water may leak through.

Ideally, you need to see a property before, during and after rain to check for these problems, which for a buyer may not always be feasible. If this is not possible, however, do look for evidence of leaks such as damp patches, water staining or mildewed areas both inside the property and on external walls. Finally, properties need to be checked for ventilation, such as air bricks, at the base of chimneys and around the lower brickwork of a building. These help to improve airflow throughout the building and reduce dampness.

Timber decay: Most properties incorporate some timber in their structure. This might be in the roof or a major component of the property. The most common area for decay is if the property has suspended timber floors. Unless there is enough ventilation, these timbers can become damp and start to rot. Signs of timber decay are not easy to spot as they tend to be hidden by floor coverings such as carpets. It will require a qualified surveyor to assess the property for the likelihood of such a problem and then a specialist surveyor/ timber company to confirm what is required and how much it will cost to fix.

Settlement: It is important to understand that all properties move to some extent over time. Even a newly built property, for example, experiences some 'settlement', but this is not the same as subsidence (see below). After a property has been built, the weight of the building compacts the land below and as a result it 'settles' by a few centimetres. Consequently, this may cause some small cracks between walls and their ceilings/floors, which, once filled, do not occur again.

Another cause of settlement might be a change from wooden to PVC windows, which might not support heavy building materials such as brick, so they 'sag' under the weight causing cracks below the window if there is no lintel.

In recent years, properties built on clay have also experienced some settlement. The weather changes have resulted in a contraction of the clay from periods of heavy rainfall followed by drought. The contracting clay has resulted in a new level for the land and some properties have therefore needed to 'settle', creating some cracks in their structure.

Subsidence: This is where a property 'moves' relative to the land it is built on. It can result in hefty cracks and the requirement for significant building work to put the problem right. This can be a pretty scary word for most buyers –

and sellers – if their property is affected. However, only a small percentage of properties are seriously affected by subsidence.

For subsidence to happen, typically there needs to be an external cause. For example, a property built over a tunnel or mineshaft is vulnerable to this problem if the ground underneath moves significantly and the property 'falls' with the land. This is a very rare occurrence, however. More commonly, subsidence may occur if the foundations of a property have been altered in some way. A tree's roots penetrating the foundations, for instance, or the collapse of a nearby drain, can lead to subsidence through damage to the foundation's structure.

Spotting subsidence in a building is best left to the professionals. However, serious subsidence usually surfaces with a 'sudden' crack that is a centimetre or more in diameter, which is something that you look out for yourself. If this happens in a property you own, contact your insurance company immediately.

In many cases, buildings insurance will cover subsidence, and once the problem has been fixed, there should be few issues with regard to purchasing the property. However, as a vendor, you alwys need to bear in mind that buyers may prefer not to purchase a property with a history of subsidence, so be aware that this may influence both the price and time it takes to sell your property.

If you have spotted any cracks in a property you are looking to buy or sell, it would be worth ensuring that a surveyor investigates these to determine the cause and recommend what needs to be done to rectify the problem.

Specific types of property

Some property types constructed in a certain way or at a particular time are vulnerable to particular problems arising. It is important to look out for these when selling or buying. This is not just because of the cost of putting them right, but because many of these require on-going maintenance.

Making your choice

The most important aspects to bear in mind when considering a property are its age and construction.

Thatched properties

If you are looking to buy an old property with a thatched roof, then be aware that a building survey is a must and unless a property is in exceptional condition there are likely to be significant maintenance issues. The thatch, for example, needs to be updated in some areas every fifteen years and this costs around £5,000. In addition, it will need to be completely renewed every 25 to 50 years at a cost of £12,000 upwards. Treatment is also required to ensure the thatch is as fireproof as possible.

Old properties

Old properties (built before the 1930s) weren't built to conform to current building regulations, with solid foundations and proper damp coursing, so a building survey is always required and, unless the property is scrupulously maintained, is likely to reveal some damp and decay. As long as the cause, treatment and attendant costs are accurately identified and the property continues to be well maintained, there should be no recurring problems.

Listed properties

Not all old properties are listed, but if they date back to before 1840, and especially before the 1700s, they are likely to be 'Grade II' listed. This means that the property is recorded by English Heritage to be of architectural and historical importance. There are therefore restrictions on what you can do to change a property both internally and externally. To make any changes whatsoever to a listed property you need to contact your local council for approval prior to doing the work. Owning a listed property therefore means that work you need to do could take longer than normal and the work required may well cost more to ensure it is in keeping with the property.

Edwardian/Victorian properties

As with all old properties, few Edwardian and Victorian buildings were built with foundations as solid as those required today by current building regulations. They have survived the test of time, however, and 'settled' onto the land, but if, for example, you want to build a double storey onto a single-storey section of building, it is likely that new foundations will be needed. Theses houses also tend to suffer from damp unless they are fitted with a proper damp course. The key attraction of this type of property is that the rooms are usually a good size and, being brick, they have good soundproofing.

1930s properties

These were the first homes built to conform to building regulations. They were the first to combine the comforts of modern living, such as good-sized rooms and indoor facilities such as bathrooms, with adequate foundations and damp proofing. They were also the first homes to incorporate 'cavity wall' insulation to retain heat in the home. The main problem to look for is that, due to their age, they may be experiencing cavity wall tie failure. A surveyor will be able to spot such problems, however, and estimate how much it will cost to fix.

1970s properties

Properties from this era were built with new technology that has not always lasted well. Galvanized windows and wooden facia boarding do not appear to have stood the test of time unless very well maintained. These issues should be identified on a survey, however. The reinforced concrete structure is also thinner than brick and as a result is less soundproof.

Environmental checks

It hasn't been easy to check on the surrounding environment of a property, but with increased awareness of the problems, plus access to the internet, this is starting to change. Government agencies and local councils are a good source of information to help you make up your mind whether to make an offer or not.

Living near water

The Environment Agency calculates that around 5 million people, living in 2 million properties within England and Wales, are in areas where there is a risk of flooding. With approximately 26 million homes in the UK, that means nearly one in ten properties is prone to flooding.

Living by water commands a premium for most properties. If you are looking at a property on a designated floodplain, however, then you need to make thorough checks on how this might affect your property. It is not just the possibility of flooding or damage to the property from the sea that needs to be considered. One particular issue is that of finance. Some mortgage lenders, for example, may not lend on a property likely to suffer water damage, and, furthermore, some insurance companies may charge high premiums or simply refuse to provide cover.

Finally, do not forget that if you have found what appears to be an idyllic location, then many other people might feel the same way too. Riverside towns and seaside resorts tend to attract lots of tourists in the summer months and over bank holidays. So before you purchase,

---

must know

Living near water
▶ If you cannot get buildings insurance for your property – you won't be able to get a mortgage either.
▶ Just because you think you are far enough away from a river or subsidiary does not mean you will not suffer water damage. Water can come from below ground, run off nearby fields as well as from the smallest tributary.
▶ If you find yourself in a property that floods, it is likely to take a minimum of six months before things get back to normal and you may not be able to live in your property during that time.

do make sure you know how busy the area might become during holiday seasons.

Living near the sea

If you are considering living next to the sea, then there are more problems than flooding to consider. These include subsidence, wind damage, erosion and so increased maintenance costs.

With global warming, there is an expectation of increased flooding from the sea, and in areas where there are threats from erosion, more properties are expected to have to be abandoned.

If you have found a property by the sea, check with the Environmental Agency and local authority what issues there are with regard to current and future flood defences. Ask, too, about any likelihood of erosion, especially if you are very close to or on the sea front.

Ask locally about how often properties need redecorating. The critical difference in maintenance costs between a house located inland and one near the sea is that you are likely to have to redecorate or fix things twice as often as you would normally. Even PVC cannot compete long term with the damaging corrosion of salt. One material to avoid in a property near the sea is any metal. Metal railings, window frames or guttering will be heavily corroded by the salt from the sea, so if you are considering buying a property with these features, you may want to consider budgeting for increased maintenance or completely replacing them.

Financial implications of living near water

In the main, most properties will be insurable, but if a property has been damaged by flooding or is considered to be at high risk, then the premiums may be too high to bear. The insurance industry has worked with the government to help identify three categories of risk. At the lowest end of the scale are those areas with effective flood barriers. Then come the areas where defences are not satisfactory, but plans are in place to improve them. The final category is those areas that are at high risk of flooding, but where there are no plans to improve the defences.

The Association of British Insurers (see page 148) provides key agreements to cover areas at risk from flooding. For example, areas that have effective flood barriers will be covered, although the premiums will increase the higher the flooding risk. In the second category, the current insurance company will keep the insurance in place for future buyers of the property, depending on the buyers' previous claim record. In the final case, however, the insurer may not be able to offer cover, but will consider each property individually. If you are thinking of buying a property in this category, it would be well worth checking the insurance before you even make an offer.

Other environmental risk factors

Landfill sites: There are three elements that typically affect the land a property is built on. The first of these relates to the previous use of the land before the property was built. For example, there are old landfill sites where toxic waste may have been buried or an old petroleum tank sunk in the ground. Most landfill sites have been made safe or appropriate action taken to ensure that a new building constructed on them does not suffer any problems as a result.

Unfortunately, it is difficult to find out about these issues prior to making an offer. To ensure that there are no problems of this kind, a local surveyor will need to look at the site or your conveyancer will need to conduct an environmental search. A further investigation only needs to be carried out if problems are highlighted – for example, if the property is found to have been built within 250 metres of a designated landfill site.

Pylons and power lines: The second issue to be aware of is the proximity of installations such as pylons, high-voltage power lines, substations and mobile phone masts. There have been many studies as to whether such installations can increase the risk of cancer or cause other illnesses, although the case has yet to be proved conclusively either for or against. They can, however, affect the value of a property, not least because some of these structures can emit low-level noise and many people would not want to have their children playing near high-voltage power lines.

Sewage works: Finally, watch out for sewage works or other sources of foul smells. Many people would think living next to a farm to be an idyllic location. However, once the fields are covered with fertilizer, you might feel a little differently about your purchase.

Checking for most of the above is best done with the help of a surveyor or by chatting with the locals about the downsides of living in a certain area. Remember that those living just down the road probably won't mention such things, whereas people a few streets away or on the other side of town might more readily tell you why they did not move there in the first place.

did you know?

Quietness counts
▶ Increasingly, people want to live in a quiet neighbourhood but close to local amenities such as a school, pub, take-away or shops. Be aware that increased traffic transporting people to the amenities or on school runs may mean that a property that appears quiet and peaceful at certain times of the day may not be so at others.
▶ Many areas near an airport have their own organization campaigning against the extension of flight paths, which can be a useful way of finding out about airport expansion plans.

Living with noise

It is important to visit a property several times a day – and night if possible – to see whether there are any noise issues. Local papers are very good sources of information as well as the local council's environmental health department, which is responsible for monitoring noise issues. The planning office can also advise you of any developments planned in the locality, such as additional housing or new roads.

If you are out at work for most of the day, a busy road might not be such a concern, as long as it is reasonably quiet at night and at weekends when you are around. In addition, the asking price of a property located near a busy road is likely to be cheaper, to reflect the noise issue.

Traffic: Most noise is created either by passing traffic or people attending local amenities such as pubs or clubs, or by neighbours who play loud music or keep a dog that barks incessantly. Unless realistically priced, properties on busy roads – particularly A roads – can take longer to sell. Ironically, some roads can be very quiet when they are at their most busy – for example, if traffic is queuing up for a major junction (although the pollution from exhaust fumes will be worse, of course). Difficult noise to live with is that of heavy lorries or fast cars speeding through the night or early in the morning. Good double glazing can do a sterling job at keeping out the noise, but remember that as soon as you step outside, you will be able to hear it.

If you are worried about noise from traffic or local amenities, then visit the property at several different times of the day. Evenings and early in the morning are a good time to check for noise, especially during the rush hour and school run times, as well as late evening if there are local pubs, clubs and take-away shops nearby.

Flight paths: These are a hot topic at the moment with many of the UK's airports looking to expand their capacity. The main noise issues to be concerned with are the frequency of night-time flights, the main flight paths in and out of the airport and where the aeroplanes are 'stacked' when queuing to land at the airport. Unless you are close to an airport, right under the jets' flight path, most double glazing will keep the noise out. The main problem is during the summertime, when people like to open their windows, or if there are many night flights, which could keep you awake.

Railways: Trains and trams can impact heavily on the noise in an area. Some areas, such as Clapham or Crewe, which are major railway junctions, need careful investigation if you intend to buy a property there. The speed and frequency of trains and trams will influence how intrusive the noise is likely to be.

must know

Environmental checklist
Is the property on or near:
- A flood plain?
- The bottom of a valley/hill?
- A landfill site (within 250 metres)?
- The sea?
- Pylons, power lines or mobile phone masts?
- A busy road/railway line?
- A bus route?
- A noisy industrial estate?
- A sewerage plant?
- A school?
- A pub or other busy local amenities such as a take-away?

Properties requiring specialist purchase and sale

There are some types of property that make buying and selling yet more complicated. For example, buying a leasehold property can increase legal fees by 20% and lengthen the purchasing time. Buying a newly built property can have serious consequences if you exchange contracts prior to the property being built – especially if you are relying on the builder finishing on time.

Buying and selling a flat

Flats or apartments are becoming increasingly popular in the UK. Many cities have experienced regeneration, turning old warehouses, industrial areas or commercial buildings into apartments.

Buying and selling flats generally incurs higher legal fees than buying/selling a house because they are leasehold. This means that you purchase the flat on the basis that someone else owns the building that the flat is in. You buy a right to live in the flat for a certain period of time and property details will specify this leasehold in terms of the number of years it has still to run. The leasehold situation is made even more complicated by the fact that new rules are being introduced. These are covered in detail in the next section.

Although the leasehold situation is, from a legal viewpoint, the main issue when buying or selling a flat, there are several other points that you need to bear in mind before you consider purchasing such a property.

Checking for noise

One of the potential problems when buying a flat is the noise from people above, below or on either side. With the current trend for laminate and wooden flooring, this is more of an issue nowadays as this type of flooring does not absorb noise, unlike fitted carpets.

The best way to check for noise from neighbouring flats is by visiting the property at different times of the day and week. You do not necessarily have to visit the property itself, but you can check for noise on the floor above or below. In addition, you could speak to the caretaker or the residents' association – which most blocks of flats will have.

A legal check on noise would take the form of 'buyer's enquiries' into any issues regarding noise from neighbouring flats. If you then move in and find there have been issues that were not disclosed when asked, this gives you legal grounds to make a claim against the vendor.

Check on additional charges

It may be a relief not to have to look after a garden or to be responsible for major maintenance of a property, but this generally comes at a price. Owning a flat usually entails two types of charge (see box overleaf).

Leasehold restrictions

When you are buying/selling a flat, you will need to obtain a copy of the leasehold agreement. This will set out the terms of your living in the property, making clear any obligations you have to the freeholder/landlord and they have to you.

There may be important restrictions in the lease concerning, for example, sub-letting either a room or the entire property. Other restrictions can include no pets or structural changes to the property. Try to find out about any restrictions of this nature before making an offer on a leasehold property, as these may affect your decision or the price that you are prepared to offer.

Financial implications

Most mortgage lenders are happy to lend money to purchase a flat. Some lenders, however, place restrictions on the percentage of mortgage they will offer if the property is part of a house conversion.

must know

Service charge

This is normally paid on a monthly basis and can be anything from a few to several hundreds of pounds per month. The charge pays for any upkeep of communal areas, including:

▶ Gardens or grounds
▶ Entrance and corridors
▶ Parking areas.

The costs cover cleaning, lighting, heating and repairs of these areas and, depending on how the service charge is calculated, can vary dramatically year on year. The level of service charge is set by the company (or freeholder) who manages the property. There are several ways that service charges are calculated and you should check the following:

▶ How is the service charge divided up?
▶ What was the service charge over the last 3–5 years?
▶ How much and why has it increased/decreased?
▶ Are any major repairs required over the next 5–10 years, such as a new roof or windows, redecoration or building repairs?
▶ Is the managing agent/freeholder reputable?
▶ Can you see a copy of their annual accounts?
▶ How quickly do they respond if something goes wrong?
▶ What emergency procedures do they have if things go wrong with the plumbing, etc.?
▶ What are the estimated charges for the next five years?
▶ If major renovation is required
  – do you have to pay upfront?
  – can you question the cost?
  – what payment options are there (e.g. can you spread them over several years)?

Note: There may be a residents' association that should be able to help with these enquiries.

Ground rent

This is usually less than the service charge and can be payable on a monthly, quarterly or annual basis. The rent generally consists of a small charge made by the freeholder/landlord for the use of the land that they own. These charges can range from a few pounds to a few hundred pounds per year, although not every freeholder/landlord charges ground rent.

In this case, a lender may require a higher deposit and only lend up to 75% of the property's value. A lender will also want to know what the leasehold length is and may not lend any money if this is less than 30 years.

Some lenders may place further restrictions on purchasing basement flats, flats in high-rise buildings and those above commercial premises. Make sure that your chosen mortgage lender is aware of the type of flat that you are looking to purchase before you commit to an offer, so they do not reject your application halfway through the process.

The insurance for buying a flat also works differently to that of a freehold property. You still need to take out your contents insurance, but the buildings insurance is the responsibility of the managing agent/freeholder – albeit that you will be charged your share. It is important that you gain the details of what the buildings insurance covers so you know if you need to take out any further insurance.

Leasehold and freehold

Land Registration Act

The law laying out the registration of land ownership is based on the Land Registration Act of 1925. In it, property is categorized as either 'freehold' or 'leasehold'. Freehold property means that the owner of the property also owns the land within the boundary declared on the title deeds.

For properties such as flats or, very occasionally, certain houses, the ownership is deemed to be 'leasehold'. This means that a property is purchased with a 'right to live' in the property and on the land for a set period of time.

When the leasehold laws were first introduced, a '99-year lease' seemed adequate. A hundred years later on, however,

did you know?

▶ The government estimates that there are over three million leasehold residential properties in the UK. Leasehold properties make a perfectly good purchase, providing all the necessary legal checks are carried out.

▶ From a financial perspective, it is important to check that a mortgage company will lend on a property with a lease of less than 70 years. Some mortgage companies will accept much less than this, but it can reduce the value of the property. In these circumstances, it may be worth investigating extending the leasehold.

there have been problems concerning the renewal of leases, with leaseholders occasionally being 'held to ransom' by the freeholders. There have also been cases where freeholders have overcharged leaseholders for maintenance work on the property. As a result, new laws are now being passed giving greater rights to the leaseholder to ensure the freeholder does not take advantage of them.

New legislation

Over the last ten years, new legislation has given the leaseholder greater ability to extend their lease or to purchase the freehold. In addition, the leaseholder now has the option for a 'right to manage' the upkeep of the property. As before, leaseholders and freeholders can go to the Leasehold Valuation Tribunal to help resolve financial disputes between the landlord and tenant. The Commonhold and Leasehold Reform Act of 2002 enforces the above changes and offers the alternative of owning a flat under 'commonhold' (a type of freehold) as opposed to time-restrictive leasehold.

must know

Leasehold checklist
● Are there restrictions/limitations on the use of the property?
● Who is the freeholder/managing agent?
● What are the contact details for the freeholder/managing agent?
● Have there been any disputes between freeholder/leaseholders?
● What are the charges associated with the property, e.g. ground rent or service charges?
● How is major maintenance work funded, e.g. for new windows/roof?
● How long is the lease?
● Can the lease be extended and if so for how long and at what cost?

Newly built properties

Buying a newly built property or 'new build' can have many advantages if the property is soundly constructed. The chief advantage is that the buying process is 'chain free'. Your purchase does not rely on someone having to find another home, or on liaising with someone who does not understand the moving process. A further advantage is that many builders offer 'part exchange' schemes. These vary in the way they work, but most offer to purchase and then sell your existing property for you, allowing you to purchase their property without a chain. This usually means that you do not have to instruct or pay an estate agent, although legal and surveying costs are still incurred.

If you buy early enough, many builders will allow you to choose the fixtures and fittings of the property and occasionally even change the layout. To do this, however, they typically require a deposit, or even an exchange of contracts, prior to the property being finished.

New builds carry the benefit of up-to-date building methods and needing to comply with the latest building regulations. This means that they can be more energy efficient and have good security and safety features such as smoke alarms and circuit breakers. They are not without their problems, however, and there are certain checks you should always carry out on the builder and property prior to making an offer (see box above).

must know

Checking your builder
If the builder is small and locally based, then you should:
▶ Ask for details of previous properties they have built and to look round, if possible.
▶ Ask for customer references.
▶ Check their financial position.
▶ Ask whether there is a complaints procedure.
▶ Request aftercare service measures.

If the property is built by a large, well-known builder, then find out who the site manager is for the new build in question and check out one of their other sites.

Warranties

Many people believe that the widely advertised ten-year NHBC or Zurich warranty means that the builder will have to pay if anything goes wrong, but this is not the case. If anything does go wrong in the first two years, you have to prove that the damages were the fault of the builder before they will agree to the repairs. After that, it is the builder who is covered by the warranty. In other words, the warranty does not give you any rights to claim against the builder, only help via the NHBC to resolve the issues. Matters are thus in the hands of the builder and warranty provider and there is little that you can do to influence the speed of the process.

Snagging surveys

Of course it is better to have the warranty than not, but the only way you can ensure the new build is finished to a high standard is to instruct an independent surveyor or arrange for a specialist survey for new builds known as a 'snagging survey'. To give an indication of how new builds can be far from perfect, one only needs to look at the survey conducted by a snagging specialist called Inspector Home (see page 149), which has been tracking problems they have found with new builds. In 2004 they recorded a variation in the number of problems within a single newly built property from six defects to over 300!

Conveyancing

If the property isn't finished before you buy it, make sure you use an independent conveyancer who is experienced with dealing with new build purchases as they should ensure that no contracts are exchanged or completed without the right clauses to protect you being put in place. These inclusions should cover what would happen if the property is not constructed to a good enough standard, if it weren't ready on time or if the agreed specifications are not included.

Financing

In the main, there is little difference between financing new build compared with a second-hand home. You may, however, need a higher level of insurance if the new build is not ready on time, and you will need to talk to an independent financial adviser or your mortgage lender/insurance company about this.

You may have to pay a reservation fee, which can range from a few hundred to thousands of pounds and might not be refundable. In some circumstances, you may have to exchange prior to the property being built. With house prices in the UK having increased so much over the last few years, it may be that you cannot fund the deposit required without having sold your own property. In this instance, the builder may help fund the deposit in the short term or accept a smaller deposit than usual. All this requires specialist support from your conveyancer and mortgage lender, so make sure that both parties are experienced in handling the purchase of new build properties before you instruct them.

Self-build properties

Over 20,000 self-build properties are constructed every year in the UK, which is more than any single property developer will build. For some people buying a plot of land and designing and building their own home can be the realization of a dream.

There are two ways of building your own property. The first is to buy one that is 'ready-made'. These come in all shapes and sizes, from modern to traditional in style. The second way to build your own property is to design and build a property from scratch, usually with the help of a qualified architect and on-site project manager. As a guide only, a self-build home in the UK, including land and building, costs around £150,000.

There are three stages to the self-build process:

▶ Finding a plot of land.
▶ Applying for planning permission to build.
▶ Building the property.

Finding a plot of land

This is often the longest stage of the process. With the increased popularity and ease of self-building, more and more people are looking to create their own living space. This, together with a shortage of land to be built on, has had a significant impact on land prices, which have risen accordingly. Many people now sell land with planning permission as this costs only a few thousand pounds to obtain, but can add tens of thousands of pounds to the land's value.

Financing land purchase

The cost of financing and purchasing land consists of the price of the land, plus associated surveys and legal fees. These can eaily add up to over £1,000. In addition, you will need to pay stamp duty on land purchases, just as you would on a property (see pages 110–11).

Planning permission

Even if you find the perfect plot of land, there is no guarantee you will be allowed to build on it. It may be that someone is selling the plot because they have not gained planning permission for a property themselves. The main contact for planning permission is the local authority responsible for the land you wish to buy. You can contact the planning department directly and ask for a view on a site's position to see if there are any obvious problems or if planning permission has been rejected in the past.

You can apply for planning permission from the local authority and there are two stages to this. 'Outline planning permission' is really only to gauge the local authority's view of your plans. They may reject them at this stage or suggest some amendments, but this may be a cheaper alternative as you can incorporate their changes into the full planning permission (the second stage).

The whole process should last approximately eight weeks, but unfortunately it can take months if there are objections raised by, for example, nearby residents. The cost of obtaining planning permission varies considerably, from a thousand pounds upwards.

Financing the build

The main barrier in the past to building a property yourself has been the financing of it. However, there are now special mortgages for self-build projects that allow you not only to borrow money to finance building your new home, but also to live in your current home until you are ready to sell and move to your new property.

Some mortgages will allow you to borrow up to 95% of the cost of the land and building, while others may restrict this to 75%. The money is not released all in one go, but at certain stages of the build, such as when buying the plot of land, adding the foundations and then making the property wind- and waterproof.

Insurance

During the building process you will also need specialist insurance to protect you – and whoever is lending you money. Known as 'site insurance', it should cover you for essential public and employee liability or accidents during the build and for rebuilding any part of the property that is damaged during the building process. This type of cover costs several hundred pounds. Further insurance would be required to cover tools, equipment and a temporary caravan or site office.

The site insurance usually covers a property for a period of up to two years. It can be extended or converted into buildings insurance once you have finished building the property. But do remember to set up any contents cover in addition once the property is habitable.

Building your own home
People often think it is easy to manage a build themselves, but this can turn into an expensive mistake as they may lack the relevant experience and not be able to visit the site on a full-time basis. Most developers employ a site manager to oversee their developments. Site managers are experienced at making sure that all the materials – and contractors – are in the right place at the right time and that the work is done to a high standard. In addition, they tend to have enough knowledge and the right contacts to resolve any problems quickly and help save money during the build.

Housing association properties

After the sale of council houses in the 1980s, housing associations were set up to own and run 'social' housing in the UK. They can also manage property stock by selling and renting to the private sector, as well as ensuring they provide for those who cannot afford to buy a property.

As a result of this change, a new way of buying and renting property has been developed known as 'shared ownership'. The associations can sell a part of the property to 'key workers', such as policemen and women or nurses, and those who cannot afford to purchase a property outright. You can purchase anything from 25% to 75% of a property, or even to buy the property outright. You then pay rent for the rest of the property to the housing association. Over and above the monthly mortgage costs, rents vary but can be up to a few hundred pounds.

Shared ownership – buying

Not everyone is eligible to purchase a property on a 'shared ownership' basis. To do so, you first need to fill in an application form. Priority is typically given to those in social housing already, first-time buyers and those on an income that precludes them from being able to purchase anything in the local area.

Not all mortgage lenders will lend on a shared ownership basis. It is best to contact your current bank or building society or a lender who has dealt with shared ownership before and will try to find you the best option. Once you have organized your finances and the percentage share of the property you are going to purchase, the housing association will advise on the rent and additional service charges that you will need to pay. From this stage, once a price has been agreed, the process is similar to that of a normal purchase. It is important, though, to ensure that you instruct a conveyancer who has experience of this type of purchase.

Shared ownership – selling

If you want to sell the property, you first have to let the housing association know. You can then either sell your share at the current market value or purchase the rest of the property and then sell outright. If the market has gone up, then you benefit from your share's increase. If it goes down, then of course you will lose money like everyone else.

Should you wish to sell your share of a property, you need to bear in mind that the housing association may have an influence on the sale price and on whom they wish to sell it to. This may be helpful, however, if they have a list of people wishing to purchase, as you may avoid having to pay estate agent fees.

The only downside financially about shared ownership is that, although you may only own 25% of the property and rent the rest, you still have to pay the full service charge and ground rent. This is no different, though, to renting a property. The benefit, however, is that if the market moves up in value, or if you want to make changes to the property to which the housing association has given its approval, it can add value to the property and hence your share.

did you know?

Shared ownership
This can be a great way of getting on the first rung of the housing ladder and buying a share of a property that tends to be well maintained by the housing association. You do need first to make sure that you are eligible and to find out about such properties early, as once they are released they tend to be sold quickly as demand is high.

Structural check

The Royal Institute of Chartered Surveyors (RICS) offers lots of help both on- and offline with regard to property problems, including useful guides on property surveys and issues such as subsidence. You can also call for help with issues to do with buying/selling property in Scotland:
tel. 0870 333 1600
www.rics.org/Property/ rics_helping_hand.htm

For free information on the different types of damp including free, downloadable leaflets and books, visit the Safeguard website. Contact:
tel. 01403 210204
www.safeguardchem.com

Specific types of property

For a wealth of information on older properties, go to:
www.periodproperty.co.uk

For information on listed properties, visit:
www.heritage.co.uk

To join a group of thatched property owners, contact the Thatched Owners Group:
tel. 01406 330007
www.thatched-group.com

Living near water

The Association of British Insurers (ABI) have a special section on their website to help you work out if you can insure a property before you make an offer or if they consider it a risk of flooding (or subsidence):
www.abi.org.uk/floodinfo

Also contact the following to see if you are at risk of flooding:
Environment Agency
tel. 08708 506506
www.environment-agency.gov.uk

Homecheck
tel. 0870 606 1700
www.homecheck.co.uk

For an online map showing the proximity of a property to water, visit:
www.multimap.co.uk

In Scotland, the Scottish Environmental Protection Agency (SEPA) operates a flood warning and information service. Log onto their website or call their Floodline:
tel. 0845 988 1188
www.floodprotectionassociation.org

want to know more?

Environmental checks

To find if your property might be affected by coal mining, visit:
www.coal.gov.uk/services/miningreports/gazetteer/englandwalesgazetteer.cfm

For help understanding the issues of living near a flight path, log onto:
www.hacan.org.uk

Leasehold and freehold

For free advice on changes in the law for leasehold and freehold, contact the Leasehold Advisory Service:
tel. 020 7490 9780
www.lease-advice.org

For impartial information on extending your lease, visit the following website, clicking on their advice and support centre:
http://england.shelter.org.uk/home/index.cfm

Newly built properties

To find a new home and for the benefits of buying a new home, visit:
www.new-homes.co.uk

For information on problems with buying a new home and 'snagging', contact Inspector Home:
tel. 0845 408 4979
www.inspectorhome.co.uk

Self-build properties

For information on buying a plot of land and building your own home, contact:

Buildstore
tel. 0870 870 9991
www.buildstore.co.uk

Plotsearch
tel. 0870 870 9991
www.plotsearch.co.uk

To obtain free guides for help with planning permission search the following website under 'Planning: A guide for householders':
www.odpm.gov.uk

Housing Association properties

To find out more about housing associations and shared ownership, contact the following organization or the housing department of your local council:

Housing Corporation
tel. 0845 230 7000
www.housingcorp.gov.uk

5 Renting a property

Most people would prefer to buy a property than to rent one, but there are times when renting can be a better option. However, knowing how much it costs to rent a property rather than to buy one is not something regularly covered by the media. So is buying really better than renting?

Buying versus renting

In the UK, we tend to be reluctant to rent, preferring to get onto the property ladder. There are two main reasons for this. First, we think that if we do not buy now, prices will rise and we won't be able to buy in the future. Second, we like to decorate and furnish our home in the way we, not a landlord, would want.

Buying a home – the disadvantages

Buying a property is an expensive business, requiring a lot of time for looking for properties, visiting them and finding one to make an offer on. Then, even if your offer is accepted, it can be months before you move in.

To purchase a home, you need to pay out money that you cannot always recover, especially if the sale falls through. To employ a conveyancer and surveyor will cost at least £1,000. Mortgage application and valuation costs have increased over the last few years and can be several hundred pounds or more. On top of this there are searches and stamp duty of at least 1% for properties over £120,000. In other words, buying an average home will cost around £5,000. On top of these costs, a 5–10% deposit needs to be found, which on an average-priced property of £150,000 can be up to £20,000. Then there is removal to consider, together with repairs, changes to fixtures and fittings, redecoration and refurnishing, all of which will further add to the costs.

Bear in mind, too, that although properties tend to increase in value over time, in the short term owners are responsible for more maintenance costs than those who rent. For example, homeowners need to pay out for buildings insurance, any renovation, updating or sorting out problems to do with the property. They also have to bear the cost of selling the property later on.

These costs can quickly mount up, with ongoing costs of owning versus renting a property being at least £1,000 more a year than for anyone who rents. It only needs a boiler to be replaced at several thousands of pounds for a property to begin to lose money for its owner in the short term.

Renting a property – the advantages

Because buying a property is expensive and can tie you down, it is sometimes worth thinking about renting first or even in between house moves. For example, if you are moving to a new area, then renting can be a good opportunity to get to know the area first and identify where you would like to live. Alternatively, you might be thinking of buying a property with someone else, but are not yet sure even if you will be able to live together. Renting in between house moves can be helpful if you want to wait for your 'dream' house to come up for sale. Also, if you have nothing to sell, you are effectively a cash buyer. This may help you gain a better price or secure the property over another buyer waiting for a sale to go through.

Renting, by comparison with buying, is much more straightforward, quick and has limited ongoing running costs. Most properties on the market are rented within a few weeks and if vacant, you can move in straight away. The costs associated with organizing a property to rent are much less than buying. There is no conveyancing or surveyor's report to contend with as contracts are usually drawn up by the letting agent and can be more easily checked by potential tenants.

Rental costs

The main costs to consider are any finding fees, although it is usually the landlord that pays to find a tenant rather than a tenant to find a property. The second cost is for the inventory – that is, a detailed list of what is in the property. This is normally done twice, once before the tenant moves in and again when they move out. Typically a landlord will pay for one inventory and a tenant for the other. A deposit is almost always required and equates to one or more months' rent. In addition, there will be ongoing costs such as council tax, utility bills and contents insurance. Once the rental price is agreed, however, and if you have a well-drawn-up contract, the rent cannot go up during the term of the tenancy unless you agree to it.

How to value a rental property

Assessing the value of a property being bought or sold is much easier than estimating its rental value. For example, there is no rental version of the Land Registry, which records prices land and property have sold for. Rental prices are measured in a similar way to property prices, but there are significant differences, some of which make it much more difficult to track the rental value of a property.

Tracking a property's rental value compared with its bought/sold value: There are no tax implications on average residential property rentals, so the government has no requirement to record the details of the price the property was rented out at. Secondly, properties can be rented out every 6–12 months or more. By contrast, properties are not normally bought and sold as frequently, so it is much easier administer as they change hands less often. What makes the issue of recording rentals even more complex is that a rental value is normally quoted by month or week, and this can change every time it is re-rented, making it even harder to track.

Many letting agents typically hold more rentals at any one time than an average estate agent would have properties for sale, yet still have a comparable number of staff and size of business. This makes the workload much higher and records more difficult to keep up to date. Many properties are also rented out without a letting agent, whereas estate agents sell most properties, so tracking rental property prices from an individual landlord is much harder to do across the market.

Finally, a landlord may decide to rent out a property at a much lower price to attract a tenant quickly. If this information is readily available, it may deter landlords from offering this discount for fear that existing/potential tenants may find out and demand the same, lower rate on a permanent basis. When buying, on the other hand, there is little that the buyer can do to complain about the price that they paid once the property has been sold.

Rental price surveys: There are, however, some measures of rental prices in the UK that can be relied upon to help identify how much it will cost to rent the type of property you are looking for. As with property price surveys (see pages 18–19), this information is crucial in ascertaining the rental prices in different areas and what you can get for your money.

The Royal Institute of Chartered Surveyors (RICS) conducts the best rental price survey nationwide. Their survey records the rental prices of one- and two-bedroom flats, three-bed semis and four-bed detached properties. The survey covers areas by region, such as the East Midlands or the Southeast, so is not specific to a road, or even local town. It does, however, give a good indication of trends in the rental market, such as rents rising or falling, and general levels of demand and supply by region.

A second survey is from a company called Paragon (one of the leading providers of buy-to-let mortgages for the investor market). Their survey, 'Buy To Let Trends', is produced quarterly, and although it is mostly of interest to landlords, it is helpful to look at to assess whether rents are likely to be rising or falling (see page 184).

good to know

Checking rental prices
▶ Two further areas of help with rental prices are the property search engines, such as Rightmove, or large letting agents such as Belvoir Lettings. By searching their websites (see page 184), you can gain a very clear idea of which agents let what type of property. For example, are their properties all geared towards the corporate and professional let, or do they specialize in properties for the family or for students?
▶ If you live in the Home Counties or certain towns around the country such as Oxford, the Find a Property search engine (see page 184), provides an excellent 'snapshot' of property rental prices by town, or in London, by postcode. This information is based on what the property was 'advertised at' as opposed to the actual rental price agreed.

What influences rental prices?

When buying, prices are influenced by the number of properties on the market and number of buyers looking at the time. The location, condition of the property, its age and character can all affect the price of a property. When people rent, however, they do not look for the same things that a buyer would.

Best-value rental

When buying, people tend to purchase as big a property and plot as they can. For renters this is 'wasted' money. They only want to pay for the size of property they need on a day-to-day basis. They are less interested in 'guest rooms' and may not want a garden to look after. The age and character of the property is less important than the condition and facilities, such as a well-equipped kitchen or an en-suite bathroom if sharing the property with another tenant.

Best rental investment

Different factors influence the rental price and it is much harder to 'add value'. What private landlords tend to do is pitch their rental properties at different markets to gain the best 'yield' on their investment. For example, buying a property for £150,000 consisting of a two-bedroom flat in a 'top' area, with a rent of £1,000 per month, is a better investment than paying £200,000 for a three-bedroom suburban house with a rent of £1,250 per month. The first property is more likely to be let to a professional couple with no children and wanting a central location and the second to a family moving to the area who are more concerned about schools and local amenities than a good night life!

Location

Location can also have a major impact on the price of rentals. Good properties in good areas near to city centres are usually higher in

price, just like house prices. Suburban and country properties –
however idyllic – do not usually command similarly high prices in
rentals as they do when being bought/sold.

This is partly due to the requirement of people who are renting
for somewhere situated near their place of work and requiring good
rail and road networks – usually in town centres. Many people who
rent in the private sector are professional couples or single people.
Those with children usually rent only if they absolutely have to, as
they would prefer to have a more stable base and additional
bedrooms increase the rental cost.

Demand for rental properties

This depends on the requirement for temporary accommodation –
and the affordability of purchasing a home. If property prices are
high, potential first-time buyers cannot buy and so tend to rent,
thereby increasing demand. In the UK, a much lower percentage of
its property stock is available for rent in the private sector compared
with most other European countries. Even the increase in buy-to-let
purchases is estimated to have only increased the private rental
stock by a few percent. So not only are we short of properties to
purchase in the UK, but only a small amount are available for rent,
hence rental prices go up when demand is higher than supply. Just
as with house prices, rental prices vary dramatically according to a
property's condition, its location and how many people want to rent
it at the time.

Who determines a property's rental value?

Selling a property is very complicated in that the estate agent,
surveyor, mortgage lender as well as the vendor and buyer each
have a view on how much a property is worth. When renting a
residential property, this is much more straightforward as it is only
the letting agent and/or the landlord who decide on the level of rent
to be advertised. It is then up to the tenant to research the market
and decide whether they offer the rent asked or try to negotiate.

If you are renting from a private landlord, they can set whatever rent they wish and you are free to negotiate with them. If you are renting from an agency, they will recommend to the landlord what they feel is the maximum rental value, based on properties previously or currently let and any offers made are likely to need to be agreed with them first.

Rental period affecting price: As with house prices, the rent agreed could go up or down depending on how quickly the landlord wants to let the property out. But this is not the only factor determining how much rent is paid. For example, it might be possible for a renter to gain a better deal if the lease is for 12 months rather than six, or indeed for an even longer period. The longer the rental period, the fewer times the landlord has to find and approve a tenant, with all the costs that this entails. The numbers of inventories required over time are reduced too, and the landlord is less likely to have the property empty at any one period of time. Remember, however, that if you are renting for more than 12 months, the landlord is likely to reserve some right to increase the rental price.

Other factors affecting rental prices: Letting agents take many factors into account when pricing a property for rent. The two most important factors are the current level of demand and the type of market that the property is aimed at (see box opposite). Locally, rental prices may rise or fall on a monthly basis depending on the type of market.

Letting agents have to really understand what properties are available at what price in the local market – much more so than estate agents – as decisions are made more quickly and the market is highly competitive. If the agent prices the property wrongly, then a potential let property may sit on the market, which is usually disastrous for the relationship between the landlord and letting agent.

Two different types of let

Student lets: With student lets there are likely to be certain times of the year that they are looking for accommodation. The start of term in September/October or in January are particularly popular dates for moving. Students may move into new accommodation after the Easter holidays, but, as this is usually exam time, it is less likely. As a result, if properties are aimed at the student market, prices could go up if demand is higher than supply before the beginning of the autumn or spring term, or down if there are too many properties for rent on the market, such as during the summer term.

Professional lets: With professional lets, people could move at any time of the year, so it is less seasonal than a student market. The main influence is value for money if they are paying themselves, or the budget restrictions placed by a company if it is paying for the move and temporary accommodation.

Rental assessment committees

If you are already renting a property and are informed that the landlord is intending to increase the rent – in your view unfairly – then it is possible to have the increase reviewed by an independent government body. However, this is only really worthwhile if you are already renting and have a tenancy agreement in place, as if you have not rented the property yet, the landlord is unlikely to want to go through the procedure.

Rental assessment committees are part of the Rent Service (see page 184), a government agency that helps to determine rents for social housing but can also intervene in the private sector. If you want to have your rent reviewed, then you can contact the local office, supplying them with information about why you think the increase is unfair, while your landlord can provide evidence to the contrary. This is all free of charge, unless either side decides to invest in further help and support.

Rental contracts and payments

When renting a property, the two most important matters to consider are the terms and conditions and the rental payments required. It is also important to understand what rights you have to renew your contract and what happens if you want to leave.

Short-term lets

A short-term let can be anything from one to six months. It is more expensive as the landlord has to keep re-renting the property and it is therefore more likely that the property will be empty for certain periods of time. Every time a new tenant rents a property, the landlord has to clean it, draw up the inventory and run checks on the tenant. Depending on the agreement with the letting agent, the landlord may also have to pay for every tenant found.

Short-term lets usually include everything that you would need to live in a property, as well as cutlery and bed linen. They usually include the utility bills too. These types of let generally take the form of 'serviced apartment blocks' owned by large property companies, although some are with private landlords.

---

must know

What the rental agreement must include
- ▶ Contact details for the tenant, landlord and/or the letting agent.
- ▶ Amount, method and date rent is to be paid.
- ▶ Any deposit monies required and under what circumstances the deposit would be withheld or paid back.
- ▶ Landlord's right to enter the property and the tenant's right to be given notice of this, plus the period of notice that would be given.
- ▶ Arrangements if any repairs are required, either in an emergency or ongoing.
- ▶ Statement about what happens if either side wishes to stop renting or letting.

In addition, attached to the agreement should be an independently assessed inventory of what is in the property and comments on the condition of the contents/décor.

Lets of 6–12 months

Most people tend to let a property for this amount of time and do so under an 'assured shorthold agreement' (see page 163). Properties are let either with or without furniture and sometimes you can replace items with your own. The landlord would normally pay for repairs to appliances and to the property and there would have to be a gas and electricity safety certificate and all furniture must meet fire regulations. The landlord and tenant would normally share the cost of the inventory for moving in and moving out.

As a tenant, you would generally have to pay for utility bills, TV licence and the council tax. Any damage to the property over and above reasonable wear and tear would also have to be paid for by the tenant.

Long-term lets

It is possible to rent a property for more than 12 months. This means there are less likely to be periods when the property is empty, thus reducing the costs for the landlord of having to find a new tenant every six months or annually. It also means that you may be able to negotiate a better monthly rental price. However, both you and the landlord are likely to want to have some 'break' clause in the agreement that allows both of you to change your mind. With long-term lets it is best to agree levels of rental increase in advance to reduce the likelihood of the landlord wanting to re-let the property year after year to enable them to take advantage of higher market rates.

What to consider when renting

When we buy a home we aim to buy the best accommodation we can afford as we hope that its value will either stay the same or increase. When renting, the more space you have and the better the location, then the more you pay. Unlike buying, there is no potential gain financially once you decide to move on.

The best option?

In some circumstances it is better to rent. There are many reasons why renting can be the best option:

- ▶ Moving to a new area.
- ▶ Short-term job contract.
- ▶ New job in a new area.
- ▶ Not cost effective to buy.
- ▶ Splitting with your partner/family.
- ▶ Seeing how well you can live with someone.
- ▶ Insufficient cash/income to purchase a property.
- ▶ Needing to wait for a particular property to come up for sale.

Space needed

When looking to rent a property, think about the minimum amount of space you'll require. There is no point paying additional rent on a monthly basis for a spare bedroom for guests when it would probably be cheaper to put them up in a nearby hotel or guesthouse when they come to stay. You should also think about whether you need a garden or not as this may be an additional cost and extra work.

How long for

When thinking about renting, you should work out how long you think you may need to rent for, how much you want to pay and whether you want to do this on a weekly or monthly basis. You also need to consider whether you want to live on your own or are happy to share with other people.

Once you have made these decisions, you can then start looking for the right type of property, in the right place and with the right rental agreement. Before you do start looking, however, you need to be aware of the different types of rental contract that you may come across. Different contracts mean that you have different rights: some give the tenant better rights than others, while others favour the landlord.

Different types of residential letting agreement

In the rental market, there are three main types of contracts in residential letting: assured shorthold, assured and regulated.

Assured shorthold agreement

For those privately renting a whole property from a landlord, the most common type of contract is the assured shorthold agreement. This agreement should include the day that you can rent the property from, when you are expected to leave, how much and when your rent is due and how the landlord would go about changing the rent. Assured shorthold agreements last for a minimum of six months, but can go on for 12 months or more.

One of the reasons for the popularity of this type of contract is that at the end of the term of the agreement, the landlord has the right to take back the property. This is a protection for landlords against people who are abusing their rights as a tenant, perhaps not paying their rent or refusing to leave. Six months is the maximum length of time a landlord would have to endure such problems – the likely time it would take to have a tenant legally evicted. If you are a good tenant, pay rent on time and look after the property, the landlord will want you to stay.

Payments under such an agreement are normally monthly and made via the

watch out!

Joint tenancy
If you are renting a property with other people, make sure that everyone's name is on the tenancy agreement – known as a 'joint tenancy' – or that you each have separate tenancy agreements. If only you sign and others cause a problem in the property or do not pay their rent, you do not want to be liable or made to leave on account of the problems caused by your co-tenants.

letting agent or directly to the landlord. It is possible, however, to agree a weekly or quarterly payment period. With a shorthold agreement, you are likely to be bound to pay rent for the fixed period that the contract states. For example, if you sign the contract for 6–12 months, you are still likely to have to pay rent for the rest of the contract unless you can negotiate for a change with the landlord or letting agent.

If you want to stay in the property beyond the end of agreed tenancy, then this should be covered in the contract. The landlord or letting agent will need to be told, preferably in writing, that the extension is wanted. If they are happy, it should be possible to extend the contract from a month to 12 months or more.

Under this agreement there are certain circumstances in which a landlord can apply to the court to evict a tenant(s) prior to the end of the contract (see box below). For the main, this includes a tenant not paying their rent, breaking their contract in some way, such as damaging the property, or becoming a nuisance to neighbours.

---

good to know

Evicting a tenant

▶ A landlord should give a minimum of two months' notice if they want the property back at the end of a tenancy.

▶ To evict someone, the time of the contract must either have finished or the landlord must have evidence that the tenant has broken the contract in some way and follow the correct legal steps. If the contract has come to an end, and the landlord has given the required notice to the tenant to leave the property, but the tenant refuses to leave, then the landlord can apply to the court to gain possession of the property.

▶ If the landlord wants to evict a tenant prior to the end of the contract then they need to:
- serve a legal notice in writing explaining in full the problem and reason for wanting to evict the tenant
- apply for a court hearing to gain a possession order
- arrange for court bailiffs to remove the tenant.

▶ Most tenants would move out after being served a legal notice, but if they do not, each step needs to be taken in order to ensure that the tenant has no case against the landlord for unfair eviction.

▶ Bear in mind that no landlord can physically evict a tenant from a property; only the bailiffs of the court can do this.

Assured agreement

This is a similar to an assured shorthold agreement, tending to be used for longer-term tenancies lasting some years instead of a few months. The basic difference is that the landlord has to take further steps to regain the property. For example, a tenant can insist on repairs being done or request a 'fair rent review' without the landlord being able to evict them, as the agreements tend to last longer than six months. Another difference is that, under the assured agreement, the spouse or partner of a tenant can continue to rent the property even if the main signatory has passed away.

There are two types of assured agreement. The first is a 'fixed term' when a specific date is set for when a tenant takes possession of the property and when a tenant must leave. The second is a 'periodic tenancy', which means that the agreement can carry on for as long as the tenant keeps paying the rent.

Payment times under an assured agreement are the same as for an assured shorthold agreement. The landlord also has the right to charge 'market rates', which means that there is likely to be a clause in the contract that allows a rent review under which rentals can be increased.

Regulated agreement

These apply only in a few circumstances, mainly if the agreement was made prior to 1989. There are key differences between assured and regulated agreements:

▶ First, the regulated agreement usually allows for the same members of the same family to carry on the tenancy agreement if anything happens to the named person on the agreement, especially if they have lived in the property for more than two years.

▶ Second, as a regulated tenant you have a right to a 'fair rent' and can therefore request a rent review by an independent third party if you are not happy with the rent increases that the landlord may have tried to put through.

▶ Finally, as long as you stay in the property, it is also possible under these types of agreement to have lodgers and sub-tenants.

The role of the landlord

Landlords are the owners of a rented property and have to ensure they abide by the law when renting out their property. They can either rent out a property themselves or employ a lettings agent to do it on their behalf. Once a tenant is in place, a letting agent can manage the property or manage the property themselves.

Legal requirements of a landlord

The main legal requirements of a landlord concern the safety of the property to be let (see box below). In 1988, new laws were introduced to help promote the private rental sector by ensuring that rental properties are safe for the tenants to live in. In addition, it is usually the responsibility of the landlord to protect the property with buildings insurance and, if they have a mortgage on the property, they will generally need to inform the lender and have their approval to rent it out.

Some landlords will only do the minimum they have to when renting out a property and certainly do not like to pay out for repairs! However,

---

good to know

Safety of a rental property
Gas and electrics: Before a property is rented out by the landlord or letting agent, the property must be checked to ensure all the gas and electrical equipment has been installed properly and is safe to use. The landlord is also required on an annual basis to ensure the boiler has been serviced. Every tenant should be supplied with a certificate from a properly regulated body such as the Corgi registration for gas and the Institute of Electrical Engineers (IEE) for electrics.

Other electrical equipment: Items such as kitchen appliances and immersion heaters or electric blankets also need to be checked to make sure they are in good working order. The instructions for how to use the equipment must be available. Checks need to be kept up to date by the landlord for the duration of the rental life of the property.

Fire safety regulations: All properties must be fitted with smoke detectors and any furniture or furnishings provided must meet fire safety regulations, amended in 1993.

Note: Never rent a property until you have seen the gas and electrical safety certificates.

most landlords do want to look after their property and know that if the tenant is looked after too, the more likely the property is to be let quickly.

Type of tenancy: Under a shorthold agreement, the landlord does not have to do much once you are in the property. However, under an assured agreement this is not the case, so it is easier to take action against the landlord if they do not fulfil their contract or try to increase the rent unfairly.

Clearly worded contract: A good landlord will have an agreement drawn up by a lawyer. It should be easy to read and make clear the important issues such as how much rent is paid, when it must be paid by and the start and finish date of the tenancy. At least 24 hours should be allowed to check it.

Who pays for what: Good landlords will also indicate what bills they pay and what the tenant must be responsible for.

Privacy: A landlord must give their tenants reasonable privacy. For example, they should not enter the property without any notice, unless it is an emergency. A reasonable time period is 24–48 hours' notice.

Repairs: It is helpful if you have a contact in case of an emergency. This may be the landlord, their nominated representative or letting agent.

Inventory: A good landlord would always get an independent party to assess a property's condition and draw up an inventory of the contents of the property prior to letting.

Landlord's rights

Landlords often request a deposit to be paid either directly to the landlord or letting agent, usually on signing the contract prior to entering the property. If at any time rent is not paid, items are broken or need replacing (beyond wear and tear), then this can be deducted from the deposit at the end of tenancy. The landlord also has a right to be paid the rent on the date that is stipulated in the contract. If rent is not paid on that date, then the landlord can put the arrears information in writing to the tenant. If there is no response or no more rent is paid, under most types of agreement the landlord can apply to the court to have the tenant evicted. This is the same if the tenant is causing a nuisance to the neighbours or damaging the property beyond normal wear and tear.

The role of the tenant

Just like the landlord, the tenant has legal responsibilities and rights, which vary slightly according to the type of tenancy agreement signed by both parties.

Legal requirements of a tenant

The tenant must, by law, abide by all clauses in a tenancy agreement. In other words, if rental of £300 per month has been agreed to be paid on the 28th day of the month and the start date of the tenancy is 1 March 2006 and ends six months later, then a tenant has to abide by this.

Tenants must also take care of the fixtures, appliances and furnishings that have been provided by the landlord. Most contracts allow for some wear and tear, but not for breakages or misuse. If there is significant damage, the landlord may have the right to retain some or all of the deposit. If anything goes wrong in the property, such as the heating, washing machine or dishwasher, then the tenant has an obligation to let the landlord know so that they can fix the problem effectively.

Finally, no tenant should exhibit behaviour that causes a nuisance to neighbours. If this does happen and the nuisance can be proved, then the landlord may have the right to evict the tenant once they have applied to the courts and won.

Other requirements

Tenants do not have as many requirements to adhere to as landlords, over and above those set out in the contract. However, a good tenant will keep a property clean and tidy, allow the landlord in at an agreed time and warn them if there are any problems with the property, appliances or furnishings.

A good tenant will make sure that they inform the landlord or lettings agent of any problems they have paying the rent and what they are going to do to rectify the problem, rather than just not pay it. On leaving, the tenant would ensure that the property was left in the same state that it was when they first rented it and make good any breakages they are responsible for.

Rights of the tenant

The main rights of the tenant relate to the legal requirements of the landlord. For example, a tenant should be given copies of any certificates to show that the gas and electrics as well as any appliances in the property have been checked and approved. These checks

should be done on an annual basis and the tenant can ask to see a record of the checks made. If the landlord is paying the utility bills as part of the agreement, they cannot just have power supplies disconnected or turned off during your tenancy.

In renting the property, the tenant is effectively buying the right to live in it on an exclusive basis, for a period of time. The tenant therefore has a right to privacy and so cannot be asked to leave prior to the departure date that has been agreed just because the landlord wants them to. Likewise, as previously stated, the landlord cannot enter the property without prior arrangement (unless in an emergency), harass the tenant in any way or try to physically evict them themselves.

Every tenant usually 'rents' the contents provided with the property, such as a cooker or washing machine. If any appliance stops working or the roof or pipes are leaking, the tenant has a right (depending on the content of the agreement) to request and expect that the required repairs be made to the appliance or the property.

Renting a room

It is generally students who spring to mind when referring to renting a room, but there are many types of tenant for whom renting a room in a house can be the best option.

Landlord's home: In some circumstances, rooms that are rented out are part of the landlord's own home. This can work well, but it does depend on the landlord. Even if the person renting knows the landlord, it is a good idea to try and get something in

Pros and cons of renting a room

Pros	Cons
▶ Good if you are moving into a new area where you don't know anyone.	▶ Won't always know your co-tenants renting other rooms in the building.
▶ Cheaper than renting a flat or set of rooms.	▶ Shared facilities.
▶ The room is usually within a larger property.	▶ Lack of privacy.
▶ Lower running costs due to shared bills.	▶ Can be noisy.

writing with regard to weekly/monthly rental charges and what notice is required to leave. In most cases, this type of arrangement is known as an 'excluded tenancy'.

Landlord's rights: If a tenant is renting a room in someone else's home, then the owner/landlord does have more rights. For example, they can charge what they like for a room and, if they have a justifiable reason, such as problems arising from living with the tenant, then they can evict the tenant themselves. Of course, they cannot use any force and may need first to apply to the court.

Tenant's rights: However, as the tenant is paying rent for the room, this means that they should have some level of privacy. The landlord cannot just enter a tenant's room when they want to, and certainly has no right to go through the tenant's personal belongings.

Shared tenancy: When looking to rent a room in a shared facility, it is important to check how private the room is. For example, is it next to the bathroom that everyone uses? Finding out the times fellow tenants come and go during the day/night is a good idea as sleep could be disturbed, especially if certain tenants are working shifts. It is also important to ask about the facilities in the house, such as the use of a dishwasher, washing machine and drying facilities. Also, check such details as whether there is enough hot water for everyone.

When sharing with other people, failing to keep shared areas clean and tidy can soon get out of hand if there is no agreement about who does what and when. So it is important to have a set of ground rules that mean people clean up after themselves or have a rota for general housework.

Paying rent and bills: When renting on a 'room only' basis, the rent usually includes most bills, such as council tax and the utility bills. The only additional bill is usually for the telephone. Do be aware also that some landlords advertise the rent required at a 'per week' (pw) or 'per month' (pm) basis, so check which is being quoted before you visit a property. From a security perspective, it is also a good idea to go accompanied or leave a list of dates and times properties are being visited with a friend/family member.

Renting or letting agents

Rental and letting agents concentrate specifically on finding tenants for landlords and managing properties on behalf of both the landlord and the tenant. There used to be either estate agents or letting agents and rarely did the two businesses mix. However, since the decline in earnings for estate agents from financial services, many have moved into the lettings market. This has also been fuelled by the growth in rental demand and the buy-to-let market. The advantage for people buying property to let is that an agency with both property for sale and for rent can advise on which properties will give buyers the best return on their capital.

As with estate agents, some letting companies concentrate on different areas within a location and on different types of rental arrangement or renter. For example, if there is a big student population, some companies may just concentrate on this market. Another market for rental agencies is professional relocation. Letting agents that focus on this market are likely to look for the relocation companies that support professional moves, as they will earn

> **must know**
>
> **Where to look for house shares**
> ▶ Some letting agents will advertise rooms in shared houses, but the owner of the property may privately advertise spare rooms. Advertisements for rented rooms can be found in the local paper in the 'private adverts' section, as well as in *Loot* and *Daltons Weekly*.
> ▶ Spare rooms are also advertised on the internet (see page 184).
> ▶ Other places to look for rooms to rent are in your local post office or newsagent's windows, or consider asking around at your place of work.
> ▶ If you are working for a large organization or going to be a student, then it is worth checking whether there is an accommodation office or department that can help you. They may list preferred landlords or companies that can help find a spare room to rent.

Checking with letting agents

▶ Rental properties come on and off the market in a matter of days or weeks, so it is important to keep in regular content with the rental agents – and there may be 20 or more that you have to keep in touch with in a large town.

▶ As properties come and go so quickly, it is hard to keep the internet sites or weekly lists sufficiently accurate and up to date. So always check directly with the letting agent or landlord that a particular property is still available.

▶ No letting agent can charge you just for giving you a list of properties available. They can, however, charge a 'reservation fee' on a property you like and also an administration fees for tenant and inventory checks.

much of their money from business that is generated by them. They are also likely to cover the more expensive end of the market.

How to find letting agents

The best way to find letting agents is to check on the internet, not just with Rightmove or other property 'portals', but also with sites that concentrate on letting, as opposed to advertising properties for sale (see page 184).

As with estate agents, there is no official regulation of letting agents and anyone can set themselves up as an agent. Be careful, therefore, that you are dealing with reputable companies as they require certain payments, such as deposits and rent, in advance.

To help find good and well-established letting agents, look for membership of either of two organizations, both of which have their own code of practice. These are the Association of Residential Letting Agents (ARLA) and the National Approved Letting Scheme. Agents registered with either of these organizations have to have the appropriate insurance in place if anything goes wrong with their business. As they could be handling tens of thousands of pounds of tenants' and landlords' money per month, proper insurance cover is clearly essential.

In addition to insurance, both ARLA and the National Approved Letting Scheme require letting agents to adhere to a code of practice or minimum level of customer service. This shows that they care about creating good industry standards and delivering a quality service to both tenants and landlords.

Costs of letting a property

Letting agents refer to their costs by a number of different names, such as 'administration' or 'referencing' fees (see box below). These costs can vary dramatically, so do check with each letting agent exactly what you have to pay for before you agree to rent a property through them.

Other charges that you need to be aware of usually relate to any breakages that you may have made and are taken out of your deposit at the end of the tenancy, unless you replace the damaged items. In addition, 'administration' charges can be made if you are late with your rent payments for any reason.

Main charges made by a letting agent

Administration fee: This is either fixed or variable, depending on how many people are renting and/or the monthly rent of the property. This fee may be a 'catch all' for the other charges mentioned below, but check what it includes before you pay it. Fees may vary from £30 to several hundred pounds.

Reservation fee: If you find a property you like, a fee may be charged to keep the property for you. This can be any amount from a fixed fee of £100 to half a month's rent. It is usually not refunded if you decide not to rent the property. As with the administration fee, this may include the cost of everything mentioned below.

Tenant referencing: This may be included in the administration or reservation fee, but if not, may incur a cost of £30 to £50 per person.

Agreement fee: Letting agents may charge you for the letting agreement that you sign. In the main, this is included in the administration fee but, if charged separately, would be around £25.

Inventory fee: This is usually split between the tenant and the landlord, or the tenant pays the 'checking in' inventory while the landlord pays the 'checking out' one. These vary dramatically but are usually from £50 to £100.

Renewal fee: If you decide to renew your letting agreement, agents may charge from £25 upwards to cover the administration of extending the agreement.

Rental agreements and services

Unlike buying a home, dealing with the legal side of renting is much more straightforward. There are three main types of rental agreement: the landlord's own, a bought agreement and a rental agent's agreement.

The rental agreement

It is very important to read an agreement through carefully. Normally they are easy to read and clearly set out what the landlord and tenant are responsible for, as well information such as the length of the tenancy. An agreement should also state what procedure a tenant should follow if they want to renew a contract or what the landlord should do if they want the tenant to vacate the property.

Most rental agents will have paid to have their own rental agreements drawn up. As with the various charges that they can make (see page 173), these agreements may vary dramatically but are usually fair to both landlord and tenant as no letting agent wants to have troublesome landlords or tenants on their books. It is unlikely that you will be able to adapt this agreement too much, but if you have any queries about any of the clauses, ask the letting agent to explain them before signing.

If the agreement is drawn up by the landlord or via their own solicitor, it is worth having this checked through by a solicitor of your own to make sure that it does not contain any 'unfair' clauses. The bought agreements are usually fine for most situations, but adaptations often need to be made for individual circumstances.

If there are any doubts about the agreement meeting your needs, or the costs that the agreement highlights, refer the matter to your solicitor. An important point to check too is whether the landlord can impose changes 'at will' or do something at their 'absolute discretion'.

Most solicitors will check a standard agreement for you within a few hours and this would cost around a few hundred pounds or less.

Other rental services

If you are renting a property directly from a landlord, you may want to draw up your own inventory to ensure you have a third party confirming the state of the property before you move in. Ask a local letting agent if they use a company that you could approach for the purpose, or you can contact certain companies through the Association of Independent Inventory Clerks (AIIC). All of their members adhere to a code of practice.

If you are intending to rent a property that is unfurnished, or has some items missing that you need during your stay, it is possible to rent or buy furniture and appliances. Companies offer 'packages' from a fully furnished option to one or two items or appliances. It is important to compare quotes as the costs can be quite high. Companies that will fit out a whole flat or house usually have a pricing package based on the number of bedrooms.

If you are buying furnishings, a one-bedroom flat can be fitted out with basic furniture from £1,000 upwards, and about the same for all the basic appliances. To rent this type of furniture and equipment would cost from £300 per month for a six-month let. Note, however, that the costs can rise to thousands of pounds, depending on the quality and size of packages.

Finally, it may be worth investing in the services of a cleaning company to ensure the property is spick and span before moving in or out or having an inventory check done. Look for local cleaning companies who offer a one-off cleaning service for a property depending on its size – and the state it is in! Prices vary dramatically but are anything from £100 up.

Step-by-step guide to renting

The stages to renting a home are much easier than buying and can happen quickly. Being prepared can make the difference between you securing the property you want – or letting someone else more organized get hold of it!

1 Choose what type of rental property you want
Before you start looking, make sure you know if you want a room in a house, a property to yourself or a fully serviced apartment.

2 Choose how long you want to rent for
If it is for less than six months, only a few options will be available so you need to visit as many letting agents as you can, or find agents that specialize in short-term lets. If you want to rent for longer than six months, be clear how long as this may help gain a reduced monthly rent or mean you are favoured over another tenant who does not want to stay as long.

3 Decide on how much room you really need
If it is one bedroom, do not waste money on two. If you want friends to stay, it would be much cheaper to pay for them to stay somewhere nearby or have a sofa bed in the living room. Check your agreement allows you to have people to stay – and for how long.

4 Work out what is the maximum you can afford each month
Don't forget to include things like council tax and water rate bills as these can cost hundreds of pounds a month, depending on the area/type of property you choose. You may also need to pay for the utilities and will have to have enough money saved for a deposit – normally 4–6 weeks' rent.

5 Research local areas to see the variation in rental prices
How much property can you get for your money? Rural properties are often cheaper than being in or near to a town and you can often get more space

too. Look on the internet and in the local weekly property paper to compare prices before choosing two or three favoured locations.

6 Make sure you have reference details
These should be your referees' names, addresses and contact details. This could be a previous rental agency or landlord, or your employer. Some institutions, such as banks or solicitors, may charge for giving a reference. It is also worth checking out your own credit rating via Experian or Equifax (see page 184) to make sure there are no bad debts that may result in a rejection of your application.

7 Make sure your money is readily available
You will need a few hundred pounds for reservation or administration fees, enough money for a deposit and some spare cash for anything you might need to purchase when you move in (such as bed linen or cutlery).

8 Visit and sign on with the local letting agents
Only do this for those that meet your criteria for a property. Make sure they can contact you at any time of the day (such as by mobile phone), that you have their latest list of available properties and any that may be available soon. Also ensure that you find out how much you will be charged to rent a property through the agency. Check the papers, internet and local post office for other rentals that might be advertised through them.

9 Visit the properties within your budget
Also make sure you constantly check what else you will need to pay for and how much it is. For example, council tax and water rates, utility bills, any ground rent or service charges or any other associated expenses. Properties in different areas can vary dramatically in the council tax and water rates they pay, so make sure you ascertain what rates these are.

10 Check the safety certificates
Having seen a property you like, ask to see the relevant safety certificates such as fireproofing, electricity and gas.

11 Check if you need to pay a reservation fee

nen choosing a property, you need to be aware that you might have to pay a reservation fee. Check the terms of the fee and under what circumstances you will lose it, or it will be refunded, before you hand the money over. Make sure you provisionally agree a moving-in date.

12 Sign an agreement

Once you have found a property, then your letting agent or landlord should give you an agreement to sign. There should be two copies, both signed by you and the landlord/their representative, and you should keep one of them for reference during and after your tenancy. Do not be pressured into signing the agreement. Have a careful read through, asking someone you trust to do the same, and if necessary ask a solicitor to check the detail for you. Particularly check that the rent you are paying is the same as that quoted.

13 Get a reference check

Make sure the letting agency has everything they need to do a reference check on you and that you sort out any queries they may have.

14 Plan for the move

Organize everything you need for removal and anything that you need for the property that it does not have.

15 Get in touch with the utility suppliers

Once you have signed the agreement and the move is confirmed, ensure that the utilities are all in your name, unless you are participating in a house share, in which case you need to make sure it is clear how much you need to contribute.

16 Draw up an independent inventory on the property

Do this prior to moving in or within the first 24 hours. Make sure that you go around with a third party so that they pick up everything you have seen.

17 Organize contents insurance

Contents insurance can be done on a room-by-room basis or for your own contents within a property.

18 Pick up the keys from the agent/landlord

Also make sure that you know how to turn off the water, gas and electricity, and ensure that you have instructions for all the appliances including the cooker, washing machine, shower and boiler.

How long does it take to rent?

Viewing rental properties tends to be much easier than viewing properties for purchase as the landlord/agency usually has the keys and if there is a tenant currently in the property, approval is usually gained easily. As a result, viewing suitable properties can take place on the same day or within a week.

References: Once somewhere has been found, most tenants' referencing can be done online, or by fax/post with tenant referencing check companies, taking only a matter of days. Employers' or bank references may take a little longer. The contracts that need to be signed are typically drawn up prior to the property being put on the market for rent, so apart from any changes that might need to be made, and once the contract has been carefully studied, the agreement can be signed. If possible, leave 24 hours just to double check everything in the contract or to ask a solicitor to check the document.

Availability to move in: Properties are either advertised as 'vacant possession' or 'available now', or they will be advertised for the time that you can move in, which may be a couple of months away. However, it is possible to agree to rent a property prior to it being free of tenants/owner. This can be a good idea if rents are rising or the market is very busy and properties are being rented fast.

Preparing for renting

Apart from the tenancy agreement, the other important piece of paperwork is the tenant references, which are crucial to all landlords and letting agents, as they need to ascertain whether tenants have a history of non-payment of rent or of causing damage to property.

Referencing checks

Referencing checks take many forms, can be quite thorough and include:

- ▶ Credit history
- ▶ Character referee
- ▶ Bankruptcy or CCJs
- ▶ Employer's reference
- ▶ Reference from tenant's bank
- ▶ Identity check (driving licence, passport or utility bill).

Guarantors

If you are renting for the first time, perhaps as a student or for a new job, it may be that you haven't yet got a credit history or even a bank account. In such cases, it is possible to offer a 'guarantor', such as a member of the family. A guarantor indemnifies the landlord/letting agent if you are unable to pay the rent for any reason or damage the property beyond the value of your deposit and cannot pay the excess.

did you know?

Address checks
These can be a problem if someone else has had bad debts at that address at the time you were living there. Make sure you alert a potential landlord/letting agency if you know that this has happened in the past.

Paying letting agents or landlords

It is a good idea to pay the letting agents fees, the deposit and rent by cheque or by direct debit so that there is an independent and clear record of what money has been paid – and when it was paid. If the letting agent/landlord is paid by cheque, it will take up to seven days for the money to clear, so this can delay moving into the property.

If a good record of the monies paid is required, a banker's draft can be given instead. This can only be produced, however, if there is enough money in the bank account and it may incur a charge of approximately £10.

Moving in

Once a property has been found, reference checks successfully completed and the right money has changed hands, then the keys should be handed over on the agreed date. The inventory check might not at first appear to be an essential part of taking possession of the property. In fact, it is incredibly important and forms part of the legal process of moving in. The inventory essentially verifies the condition of the overall property and any fixtures and fittings that are there. Hence the checks should include:

must know

Preparatory checklist
● What is your minimum/maximum time for renting?
● How many and what rooms do you require?
● What storage do you need?
● What is your total monthly budget?
● Is your credit rating good?
● Do you have enough money instantly accessible to pay for a deposit and administration fees?
● Do you have insurance for your belongings?

▶ Meter readings.
▶ Garden statues, sheds, outbuildings.
▶ Interior condition.
▶ Decorative order of the property.
▶ Condition of doors, windows, curtains/blinds, ceilings, walls and carpets.
▶ Furniture and other contents (but not expendable items such as magazines or living plants).

It is important, however, to note that lofts, cellars or other difficult-to-reach areas area unlikely to be checked.

Some inventory companies or clerks take photographs during the inventory check so that there is no doubt about the condition of the property before or after the tenancy. Ideally, go around with the inventory specialist (see page 175) so that you are sure that they have picked up anything that you also think might be wrong with the property.

Independent inventory checklist
If you are doing your own inventory check, go around with the landlord if possible and take photos as evidence of the condition of items/any damage prior to moving in. In addition, do the following:

- Check for marks on the walls, ceilings, floors, curtains/blinds.
- What appliances are there in the property, and in what condition, e.g.
  - cooker, microwave, washing machine, dishwasher
  - smaller electrical items such as kettle, coffee machine, stereo, television
  - radiators/storage heaters, boiler, water tank, fire places.
- Check each room, itemize and record the condition of the light fittings, lamps, furniture, mirrors, linen/throws, cushions, ornaments, pictures, bin, rugs, electric sockets.
- Check what cleaning equipment there is and in what condition, e.g. hoover, mop and bucket, cloths/dusters, iron, ironing board, clothes dryer.
- In the kitchen and bathroom check for:
  - cracks or marks on the sink/bath
  - utensils, crockery, saucepans
  - toilet holder, brush, shower/bath mat.

Living in a rented property

Most landlords/letting agents will want to carry out checks on the property from time to time. They have a right to do this, but must give you formal notice either via a phone call or in writing. Usually, there will be one check within the first few weeks or months and further checks every 3–6 months.

What can go wrong

If a property is rented out in good condition and well looked after, then things are unlikely to go wrong during a tenancy. However, accidents do happen and things do malfunction or break down. The tenant has a duty to let the letting agent or landlord know of any problems and – depending on the contract – the tenant has a right to have them fixed satisfactorily.

Emergencies

In the case of an emergency such as a water or gas leak, fire or flooding, then the letting agent/landlord must be contacted, even in the middle of the night. All tenants should have a 24-hour emergency number to call. Obviously in the case of a fire or break-in, the relevant emergency services will need to be called first. Make sure that you leave these numbers and your tenancy agreement to hand so that you can contact anyone in case of an emergency.

Moving out

When it comes to moving out of a rental property, it is important to be aware of any notice that has to be given. If your agreement is an assured shorthold tenancy (see page 163) that expires after six months, then the tenant has to leave on the end date, unless other arrangements have been made. If your agreement has a required notice period to leave, it is best to give this in writing to the letting agent/landlord so that there is no confusion over whether you are leaving or staying.

Further inventory check

Once notice has been given, then a further inventory check will take place. This is normally done the day before or on the day that the tenant moves out. As with the initial check, it is worthwhile being there for this so that you can be clear if there are any issues that might mean you do not get your full deposit back.

Tenancy deposit scheme

Most disputes between landlord and tenant involve the return of the deposit – or not! Due to the number of problems that arise, there is now an arbitration scheme that has been set up and more legislation to help the tenant get their deposit back. This is known as the 'tenancy deposit scheme' (TDS) and the new legislation forms part of the Housing Act of 2004.

The TDS is currently run by the Housing Ombudsman Service (see page 184) and covers landlords who are part of the service. The scheme is free and a tenant can approach the service if they feel a landlord is unfairly holding their deposit. One of the future tasks of the Housing Act will be to implement a TDS nationwide. Until then, if a landlord or letting agent does not belong to this scheme, then for help in getting your deposit back you can seek arbitration with Alternative Dispute Resolution (see page 184) or via the small claims court.

Rental price surveys/letting agents

Find the latest national changes in rental prices from the Royal Institute of Chartered Surveyors (RICS) at:
www.rics.org.uk (click on 'property', 'residential' then 'market')

Visit the website of Paragon and look in their reference area, then on their latest news articles for the latest rental prices:
www.paragon-mortgages.co.uk

Research current rental prices and letting agents in the area you are searching by looking at:
www.belvoirlettings.co.uk
www.findaproperty.co.uk
www.fish4homes.co.uk
www.primelocation.co.uk
www.rightmove.co.uk

Rental assessment committees/legal rights

If you have a dispute over the amount you pay for rent, then contact the Residential Property Tribunal Service:
tel. 0845 600 3178
www.rpts.gov.uk

For fair rent determinations and rental valuations, contact the Rent Service (an executive agency of the Department of Work and Pensions):
tel. 020 7023 6000
www.therentservice.gov.uk

For information about your legal rights when renting any type of property, contact the Community Legal Service Direct:
tel. 0845 345 4345
www.clsdirect.org.uk

Short-term lets

Hamptons have a wealth of information about short-term lets and help for tenants and landlords about renting in general:
www.hamptons.co.uk

Where to look for house shares

Visit the following websites:
www.roomsforlet.co.uk
www.spareroom.co.uk

Your own inventory

Association of Independent Inventory Clerks (AIIC)
tel. 01276 855388
www.aiic.uk.com

Your credit rating

Experian
tel. 0800 656 9000
www.creditexpert.co.uk

Equifax
www.equifax.co.uk

Tenancy deposit scheme

For information on the tenancy deposit scheme, contact the Housing Ombudsman Service:
tel. 0845 7125 973
www.ihos.org.uk

Alternative Dispute Resolution (ADR) is a government-backed scheme to help people resolve disputes quickly and cost effectively. There is a national helpline (see below) that will direct you to a panel of mediators. The costs depend on the size of your claim but starts at £250 (which is divided between the parties):
tel. 0845 603 0809
www.adr.gov

Glossary

administration fee: Fee charged by a letting agent or a landlord for the paperwork involved in renting out a property, such as tenant checks, the rental agreement and/or inventory checks.

agreed price: The price at which a vendor agrees to sell their property to a buyer.

APR: This stands for 'annual percentage rate'. It is the amount of interest (and any other cost) you pay on money you borrow, calculated on a yearly basis and expressed as a percentage of the loan.

asking price: The price at which a property is advertised or marketed by an estate agent.

average house price: An average house price does not exist for an individual property; it is a statistical term relating to the average price of all property transactions recorded.

Bank of England: The bank that sets interest rates, issues bank notes and helps to ensure the financial system remains stable.

base rate: The interest rate set by the Bank of England that UK banks must pay to borrow money themselves and from which they set their charge to consumers for lending money.

bid price: The price submitted for a sealed bid on a property in Scotland.

building regulations: The construction and safety standards set and monitored by Building Control for a new building, extension or renovation of a property.

buildings insurance: Insuring a property against fire, wind or accidental damage. This needs to be in place at the time of exchange on the property you are purchasing.

buy-to-let property: A property bought by an individual or company with the intention of letting it out to tenants.

capital gains tax (CGT): This is the tax that is incurred on any gain from the sale of an asset, such as a second home. The main place of residence is exempt from CGT.

case management: The organization and progress of legal aspects of a property sale.

cavity wall tie: The metal tie that links the outside wall with an internal one.

CCJs (county court judgements): These are incurred if you have borrowed money and then defaulted on payments to the extent that the lender has to take you to court. CCJs stay on your credit file for six years.

ceiling price: The top price that a property will be able to sell for, whatever changes are made to the property.

commonhold: This is an alternative way of owning properties that are currently or would normally be leasehold. Commonhold allows freehold ownership of a flat where flats in a block are given commonhold status. This is likely to apply to new blocks of flats, but in certain cases leaseholders can apply to the freeholder to gain commonhold status. In the future, leaseholders can set up their own organization or association to manage the building. There will be no time limits as currently imposed by the freeholders of the property on leaseholders.

comparables: Different sets of estate agent details for similar properties that help to determine an asking or offer price.

conveyancer: A solicitor, or someone within a legal firm licensed to perform the task, who carries out the conveyancing for the buyer/seller of a property.

exchanging contracts/exchange: The first major legal step in buying and selling a home. Contracts are signed but not dated and this is the first time in the buying/selling process that the transaction is legally binding.

excluded tenancy: The type of tenancy given when a tenant rents a room in the property where a landlord also lives.

fair rent: A monthly rental charge that is in line with market prices.

final sale price: The price that a property is actually sold for.

fixtures and fittings: Everything in the property that is not structural, such as light fittings, doors, windows, shelving, curtains, carpets.

freehold: The legal ownership of a building and the land it sits on.

guide price: The price at which properties are marketed in Scotland. Properties can be sold for up to 40% more that the guide price, depending on market conditions.

ground rent: The amount of money that is paid by the leasehold owner of a property to the freeholder.

home information packs: Pending legislation, these packs will contain much of the information required to purchase a property prior to marketing it, such as property searches, title deeds. The aim is to speed up the time it takes from offer to completion.

house price to earnings ratio: A statistical measure that looks at an average house price versus the average income. The higher the average house price compared to income, the more difficult it is for people to buy a property as lenders restrict mortgages to 3–4 multiples of an individual's income.

income multiple: Used by mortgage lenders to give a guide on how much money they will lend you. For example, a standard income multiple loan is three times one's salary.

indemnity policy: An insurance policy to protect the owner of a property against problems with the property's title of ownership, such as restrictive covenants.

independent financial adviser (IFA): An IFA has no restrictions on which financial packages they can offer a client.

intermediary: Typically, this will be a finance company that works with lots of lenders or insurance companies to provide consumers with a product that best suits their needs.

inventory: A record of what is in a property and its condition prior to a tenant taking possession and again when they leave.

joint agency: This applies when a vendor requests their property is marketed via more than one estate agent.

joint tenancy: Applied to renting, this means that all tenants who sign a joint tenancy are responsible for the rent/other charges whether one tenant defaults or not. Applied to buying, it indicates that you have an equal right to ownership of the property. It is the type of agreement usually set up for married couples or those in a long-term relationship. If one dies the other inherits their share.

landfill site: A site previously used for burying household and industrial waste.

Land Registry: The organization that holds the records of who owns what property/land across England and Wales.

leasehold: Ownership of a property from a freeholder that typically has a time restriction placed upon it.

mortgage: A fixed-term loan to fund the purchase of a property.

mortgage agreement in principle: The

amount a mortgage lender will offer to buyers based upon a basic assessment of their income and what they can afford, without being given the address or detail of a specific property. It is not a firm 'offer' but gives an indication to vendors and agents whether you are able to afford a property you wish to make an offer on.

mortgage valuation: The mortgage lender's assessment of a property's value on which they base their mortgage offer. The valuation is not a survey.

office copy entries: These are obtained by the conveyancer and are copies of the title deeds held by the Land Registry that confirm who owns the property and land.

property specification: This is the detail of the type and characteristics of a property that you give to an agent, such as a house/flat, number of bedrooms (plus whether single or double), number of reception rooms (living room/dining room/study), garden, garage/off-street parking.

repossession: This applies when the owner of a mortgaged property defaults on paying the mortgage and the lender has to gain possession of the property and sell the asset to pay off the initial loan.

reservation fee: The fee that a tenant sometimes has to pay to ensure a rental property is kept for them and not rented to someone else while the administration process is taking place.

reserve price: A term mostly used at auctions, indicating the minimum price a vendor will sell a property for.

sales particulars: Normally produced by the estate agent, these summarize what the property for sale consists of (number/size of rooms; features within the rooms; garden and other external features) and normally include pictures and floor plans.

sealed bids: Offers on a property that are given at a set date and time, usually to an estate agent, in a sealed envelope. They are opened together and normally the highest bid wins.

searches: A property search usually includes a search from the local council to check on any environmental issues relating to the location of the property or likely transport changes that might impact on its value.

service charges: Charges made on flat owners or tenants to pay for repairs and shared areas such as hallways or communal gardens.

shared ownership: Offered by housing associations to help people get on the property ladder. Shared ownership of properties is usually offered at 25%, 50% or 75% of the property's value.

snagging list: Defects noted on a newly built property prior to moving in.

sole agency: This applies when a vendor agrees that only one agent will market a property on their behalf.

tenants in common: This applies when more than one person owns a property. When one of the owners dies, ownership of their portion of the property passes to whoever is specified in the will, irrespective of who is living at the property.

title deeds: The record of the transfer of property from one owner to another.

under offer: The stage between a vendor accepting an offer on a property and contracts being exchanged.

vacant possession: When a property is available to let or sale with no one currently living in it.

Further addresses

Key buying, selling and renting websites
For government advice to the general public on moving home, visit:
www.direct.gov.uk

A property website that covers all aspects of property within the UK:
www.designsonproperty.co.uk

A government website advising on buying goods and services:
www.consumerdirect.gov.uk

Problems buying, selling and renting
If you have problems moving home, then visiting your local Citizens Advice Bureau (CAB) might be helpful, or log onto one of their websites:
www.adviceguide.org.uk
www.cas.org.uk

A partner website to that of the CAB is that of the Community Legal Service Direct, an organization that you can also telephone:
tel. 0845 345 4345
www.clsdirect.gov.uk

Key associations for helping with moving
Association of Residential Letting Agents
Maple House, 53–55 Woodside Road, Amersham, Bucks HP6 6AA
tel. 0845 345 5752
www.arla.co.uk

British Association of Removers (BAR)
3 Churchill Court, 58 Station Road, North Harrow HA2 7SA
tel. 020 8861 3331 (general enquiries)
www.removers.org.uk

The Council for Licensed Conveyancers (CLC)
16 Glebe Road, Chelmsford, Essex CM1 1QG
tel. 01245 349599
www.theclc.gov.uk

Housing Corporation
Maple House, 149 Tottenham Court Road, London W1T 7BN
tel. 0845 230 7000
www.housingcorp.gov.uk

Housing Ombudsman Service
Norman House, 105–109 Strand, London WC2R 0AA
tel. 0845 7125 973
www.ihos.org.uk

The Law Society in England
Ispley Court, Berrington Close, Redditch B98 0TD
tel. 0870 606 6575
www.lawsociety.org.uk

The Law Society in Northern Ireland
Law Society House, 98 Victoria Street, Belfast BT1 3JZ
tel. 028 90 231614
www.lawsoc-ni.org

The Law Society in Scotland
26 Drumsheugh Gardens, Edinburgh EH3 7YR
tel. 0845 1130018 / 0131 225 2934 (client relations office helpline)
www.lawscot.org.uk

National Approved Letting Scheme
Tavistock House, 5 Rodney Road, Cheltenham, Glos. GL50 1HX
tel. 01242 581712
www.nalscheme.co.uk

National Association of Estate Agents (NAEA)
Arbon House, 21 Jury Street, Warwick, CV34 4EH
tel. 01926 496800
www.naea.co.uk

Ombudsman for Estate Agents
Beckett House, 4 Bridge Street, Salisbury, Wilts
SP1 2LX
tel. 01722 333306
www.oea.co.uk

Royal Institute of Chartered Surveyors (RICS)
RICS Contact Centre, Surveyor Court, Westwood
Way, Coventry CV4 8JE UK
tel. 0870 333 1600
www.rics.org.uk

Home-moving charities

Shelter is an organization that works to help
people find a home. They have developed an
excellent advice and support area regarding all
aspects of buying, selling and renting a home:
88 Old Street, London EC1V 9HU
tel. 0808 800 4444 (free housing advice
helpline)/020 7505 4699
www.shelter.org.uk

Furniture Re-use Network collects furniture
and appliances for free to pass them onto
people in need:
48–54 West Street, St Philips, Bristol BS2 0BL
tel. 0117 954 3571
www.frn.org.uk

Trade shows

These run throughout the year and around the
country and include lots of companies and
seminars offering advice on all aspects of
owning or renting a property:

Home Building and Renovating Show –
throughout the year, various locations
nationwide:
www.homebuildingshow.co.uk

Homebuyer Show – end of February, in London
and Manchester:
www.homebuyer.co.uk

Ideal Homes Exhibition – end of March or
October, in London:
www.idealhomeshow.co.uk/Exhibition/Default.
aspx

Property Investor and Homebuyer Show –
throughout the year, various locations
nationwide:
www.propertyinvestor.co.uk/

For more details, contact Homebuyer Events:
tel. 020 8877 3636
www.homebuyerevents.co.uk

Television programmes

There are lots of programmes on the television
covering buying, selling, renting through to self-
build and property renovation. Some of the
longest-running and most helpful are:
Homes under the Hammer (BBC One)
To Buy or Not to Buy (BBC One)
Grand Designs (Channel 4)
Location Location (Channel 4)
Property Ladder (Channel 4)
House Doctor (Channel Five)

Index

address, change of 88, 89, 101, 119
advertising 72, 73
apartments *see* flats
assured agreement 165
    shorthold 163-4
    auctions 76-7, 81

builders 37, 141
building regulations 42
bungalows 10
buy-to-let 16, 28, 155, 157
buyer put-offs 94
buyer's questions 110, 137
buying agent 77-8, 81

capital gains tax 111
cash back offers 107
chains 90-91, 92, 118, 141
children 88, 157, 179
Citizen's Advice Bureau 81
cleaning 89, 96, 117, 175
clear-outs 88, 95
completion 58, 87, 88, 89, 118
commonhold 140
contact details 99, 100
contract of sale 98, 110
    see also exchanging contracts
conveyancing 72, 142
    choosing firm 56-9, 80, 86
    costs 58-9
    paperwork 100, 108-11
council tax 89, 101, 119, 154
credit rating 103-4, 119, 184

damp 124-6, 148
deposit 16, 87, 103, 143, 152
    rental 154, 167, 183, 184
DIY moving 44, 72-5, 81

Environment Agency 130, 131
environmental factors 33, 35, 68, 119, 130-35, 148
estate agent 36-7, 38, 45
    and chain 92-3
    charges 50
    choosing 46-51, 80

legal requirements 46, 72-3
    specification 84, 86
    valuation 30-31, 35, 46, 85
evicting tenant 164, 167
exchanging contracts 58, 66, 87-8, 90, 93, 100, 143

finance, *see* mortgage
Financial Services Authority 52, 67, 119
first-time buyers 16, 157
fixtures and fittings 108-9, 141
flats 11, 136-9
flight paths 135, 148
flooding 33, 68, 130-31, 148
'for sale' sign 72
freehold 139-40, 148
furniture, renting 175

garden 96, 122, 162
ground rent 138, 147
guarantor 180

home, preparing 94-7
home condition report 63
home staging 78-9, 81, 97
homebuyer information pack 98
house shares 169-71, 184
housing association 11, 146-7, 149

identity, proof of 98, 100
independent financial advisor 49, 52, 55, 66-7, 104
insurance 62, 70, 74-5, 99-100, 143
    buildings 33, 34, 66-7, 127, 130, 139, 166
    contents 66-7, 154, 178
    costs 69
    flats 139
    flood risk 132
    site 145
insurance company 66-9, 80-81
interest-only mortgage 105
interest rate 15, 16, 25, 104, 106, 107

internet 72, 73, 130
inventory 153-4, 167, 175, 177, 181-2, 183, 184
investment 16, 26, 28-9, 39, 156

joint tenancy 107, 163

keys 117, 118, 179

land 144
Land Registration Act 139-40
Land Registry 19, 21, 28, 87, 89
landfill sites 35, 68, 132-3
landlords 166-7
layout 122-4, 141
leasehold 101, 136-40, 148
legal firm, *see* conveyancer
letting agents 171-3, 177, 184
licensed conveyancer 57
listed properties 128-9, 148
location 84, 156-7

mail 88, 119
maintenance 128-9, 131-2, 152-3
mortgage 15, 16, 74-5, 99, 119
    flats 137-9
    interest 25, 104, 153
    multiple application 107
    offers 105-7
    organizing 102-7
    self-builds 145
    shared ownership 147
    types 103, 104-7
mortgage broker 52, 54-5, 104
mortgage company 52-5, 66, 86
    valuation 30, 32-3, 35
moving day 88-9, 181

negotiation skills 115
new builds 11, 141-3, 148
noise 119, 123, 134-5, 136-7

off-set account 106-7
offers 30, 48, 74, 86, 112-15
older properties 9, 68, 128, 148
overlooked property 123

paperwork 87, 98-101, 108-11, 119, 180
parking 122
pets 88, 179
planning 42, 134, 144-5
power lines 133
price survey 18-23, 37, 38, 85
rental 155, 184
property forms 87, 93, 98, 108-9
property market 13, 36, 91
crashes 14, 15-17, 154
local 6-7, 25-7, 36
Property Misdescriptions Act 46, 48, 50, 73
property prices 6, 18-27
property types 8-11, 26-7, 84, 128-9

railways 135
reference checks 178, 180
regulated agreement 165
regulation 42, 52, 63, 66-7, 166-7
removal 88
choosing firm 70-71, 81, 87
costs 71
DIY 75, 116
packing 89, 116-17
paperwork 101, 117
preparing for 116-18, 119
renovation 37, 42, 97
rental assessment committee 159, 184
renting 7, 92, 151-84
advantages 152-3, 162
costs 152-4
rental agreement 160-61, 167, 174-5, 178

rental prices 154-9
rooms 169-71
tenant's role 168-71
types of tenancy 163-5, 167
repayment mortgage 104-5
reservation fee 143, 178
RICS 29, 34, 63, 148
price surveys 19, 20-21, 155

safety certificates 166, 177
sales particulars 72, 96
schools 26, 29
searches 109
seaside homes 130-32
second property 68, 111
self-builds 143-6, 149
self-certification 103
self-employment 102-3
service charge 138, 147
settlement 126
sewage works 133
shared ownership 146-7
showing viewers around 74
site manager 146
snagging survey 142
social housing 10-11, 146-7
solicitor 49, 56-9, 175
space 97-8, 162
stamp duty 110-11, 119, 144
step-by-step guides: purchase and sale 84-9
renting 176-9
storing belongings 79, 81, 95
structure 124-9, 148
subsidence 33, 35, 68, 126-7
sun, orientation to 122
supply and demand 25, 157

surveyor 45, 49, 62-3, 80
surveys 30, 32-5, 87, 98
buildings report 34, 35, 60, 62-4, 124
cost 63-5
gas and electrical 35, 39
homebuyer's 34, 35, 37, 60, 62, 64, 124
independent 33-4, 124
mortgage lender's 32-3, 63-4
paperwork 100
snagging 142
specialist 33, 62, 65, 126, 142
valuation 34-5

tax 110-11, 119, 154
tenancy deposit scheme 183, 184
tenants, see renting
thatched cottages 9, 128, 148
timber decay 126
time frame 90-93, 179
title deeds 108
traffic 134-5

utilities 88, 89, 101, 178

value 13-39, 84-5, 119
maximising 27, 97
professional valuation 30-35, 46, 85
rental value 154-5, 157-8
viewings 74

warranties 141-2
water, living near 130-32, 148
waterproofing 125

Acknowledgments

The author would like to thank:
Helen Cooper from Helen Cooper Associates for her editing advice; Mark Spurling, RBS Associates, Hometrack Nationwide, Halifax and the Council of Mortgage Lenders for information on house prices and finance; Karen Babington at Easier2Move for legal information; the Royal Institute of Chartered Surveyors, Ian Pendred at Countrywide Surveyors, BuildStore and Vanessa Ambler at Inspector Home for housing information; Hamptons, www.rentchecks.com and the Association of Independent Inventory Checks for renting/letting advice; and the Shore Porters Society for removals information.

⚙ Collins need to know?

Look out for these recent titles in Collins' practical and accessible **need to know?** series.

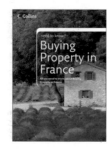
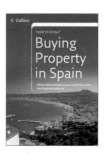

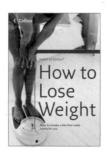

Other titles in the series:

Birdwatching	Kama Sutra	Weddings
Body Language	Knots	Wood-Working
Card Games	Pilates	The World
DIY	Speak French	Yoga
Dog Training	Speak Italian	Zodiac Types
Drawing & Sketching	Speak Spanish	
Golf	Stargazing	
Guitar	Watercolour	

To order any of these titles, please telephone 0870 787 1732. For further information about all Collins books, visit our website: www.collins.co.uk